COPYRIGHT NOTICE ....

A POTTED HISTORY ....

MALLORCAN MODERNISM ......

THE MAPS 3

THE WALKS 5

CLOCK WATCHING 6

WALK 1 - THE MAIN SIGHTS 7

WALK 2 – THE QUIETER SIDE OF PALMA 111

DID YOU ENJOY THESE WALKS? 145

INDEX 146

Copyright Notice

ISBN: 9781980551683

Strolling Around Palma by Irene Reid

All rights reserved. This book may not be reproduced in any form, in whole or in part, without written permission from the author.

The author has made every effort to ensure the accuracy of the information in this book at the time of going to press and cannot accept responsibility for any consequences arising from the use of the book.

Book Cover

Photo Casal Balaguer by Irene Reid

Enhanced by Prisma Photo Editor

A Potted History

The experts tell us that man has lived on Mallorca since about 2500 BC. If you explore the island, you can find the mysterious Talaiotic digs and sites from that time.

Some two thousand years later, the Greeks and the Carthaginians sailed in and set up busy trading posts on Mallorca. Palma, however, kicked off as a Roman settlement when the mighty Roman army took control of the island in the second century BC.

Christianity arrived in the 4th century, but later the Roman Empire fell, and the island became prey to various invaders. It became home to the Saracen pirates and the Berbers from North Africa. They attacked any passing Christian ships, and there were plenty to choose from as the island lies on the trade routes of Pisa, Genoa, Barcelona, and many other maritime cities.

Life on Mallorca didn't return to stability until the arrival of the Moors in 902 AD from Spain. The Moors, who at the time ruled most of Spain and Portugal, were far more advanced than the Christian countries to the north. Palma was a prosperous city full of markets, palaces, and mosques.

Not surprisingly Christian eyes turned to wealthy Mallorca and plans were made to retake the island. King Alfonso II of Aragon tried but failed in the twelfth century, and it wasn't until the thirteenth century that his grandson, King Jaume I of Aragon, planned his offensive. Mallorca was a tempting prize as it was not only wealthy and an important trading post to the East, but it was also held by the Moors from Spain. The Christians of the North were slowly retaking the Iberian Peninsula back into Christian control and the Balearic Islands would of course follow the same fate.

King Jaume was a religious man who believed it was his duty to lead that battle. He was backed by the church but also by members of his court who could clearly see the financial gains to be made. He was helped by both the Templar Knights who had the Balearic Islands on their wish-list, and by fleets from all over Christian Europe. The Armada landed in Mallorca in 1229.

The Christians won the immediate battle, but the surviving Moors fled to the mountains in the north and managed to hold out for another two years. Finally, they were conquered, and Mallorca became Christian once more.

Palma had an important Jewish community – the historians think that they arrived in Palma in the fifth century. They always lived in the "Jewish Quarter" but its location in Palma changed over the centuries. Even after the Christian conquest, the Jews were allowed to trade with Christians, although at night the gates of the Jewish Quarter were closed. This state of affairs came to an end in the fourteenth century - the Mallorcan Christians followed the lead from mainland Spain and persecuted the Jews until they left the island or converted.

The island was devastated by the bubonic plague in the seventeenth century, when it also had to endure the delights of the Spanish Inquisition. The converts who still lived in the Jewish Quarter were persecuted, as the Inquisition did not really believe in their conversion and found it easy to blame them for the plague and any other misfortune that befell the island.

At the start of the 19th century Mallorca started to modernise and join the industrial world - the railway arrived, and factories appeared. Mallorca's ruling class was very much on the side of General Franco when the Spanish Civil War started, and the island was always in the Nationalists' hands. The Republicans did try to take the Balearic Islands, but they failed.

Once Franco died, life started to return to normal all over Spain. Tourism arrived and quickly became the island's main money generator.

Mallorcan Modernism

As you explore you will see not only Palma's old town with its narrow streets and town houses, but many examples of Modernism – an architectural style which sprang up at the start of the twentieth century and was quite different from its classical predecessors.

Catalonia was a hotbed of Modernism with famous architects like Gaudi re-imagining the buildings of Spain. Gaudi worked on Palma's cathedral for a time and kick-started a fascination with the style, which resulted in many modernist buildings springing up in the period up to World War I.

The Maps

There are maps sprinkled all through the walks to help you find your way. If you need to check where you are at any point during a walk, always flip back to find the map you need.

The Walks

There are two walks to enjoy:

Walk 1 – The Main Sights. It takes you from the Cathedral to Plaça d'Espanya and back again. This walk covers the main sights of Palma. (4.5 km)

Walk 2 – The Quieter Side of Plama. It takes you from Plaça de Santa Eulàlia to the quieter less touristy part of Palma, including what's left of the Jewish Quarter. Then return to Plaça de Santa Eulàlia. (2.5km)

See Palma in a Day

If you are in Palma for just one day, then tackle Walk 1 which starts and finishes near the Cathedral.

If you arrive by bus or train into Plaça d'Espanya for the day, you can start Walk 1 from there instead on Page 64. Once you reach the end of walk 1, you can make your way to the Cathedral which is just a short distance away. Pick up the start of the route from Page 7. From there you can follow the first half of the walk and end up back at Plaça d'Espanya.

Clock Watching

Opening hours are always a hurdle for the dedicated explorer who wants to spend the entire day sightseeing.

As a general rule morning visits are your best bet. Churches will be closed to tourists on Sundays, and some will also close in the afternoons. Museums are best visited during the week as on Saturdays they close at 14:00 and will probably be shut on Sunday and Monday.

If you plan to have lunch at the Mercat de l'Olivar on walk 1, be aware that it closes at 14:00 during the week and is usually closed at the weekend.

Walk 1 - The Main Sights

This walk starts just outside Palma's Cathedral which is made of golden sandstone.

It's closed to tourists all day Sunday and Saturday afternoon. It doesn't open until 10 am, so you have plenty of time for breakfast.

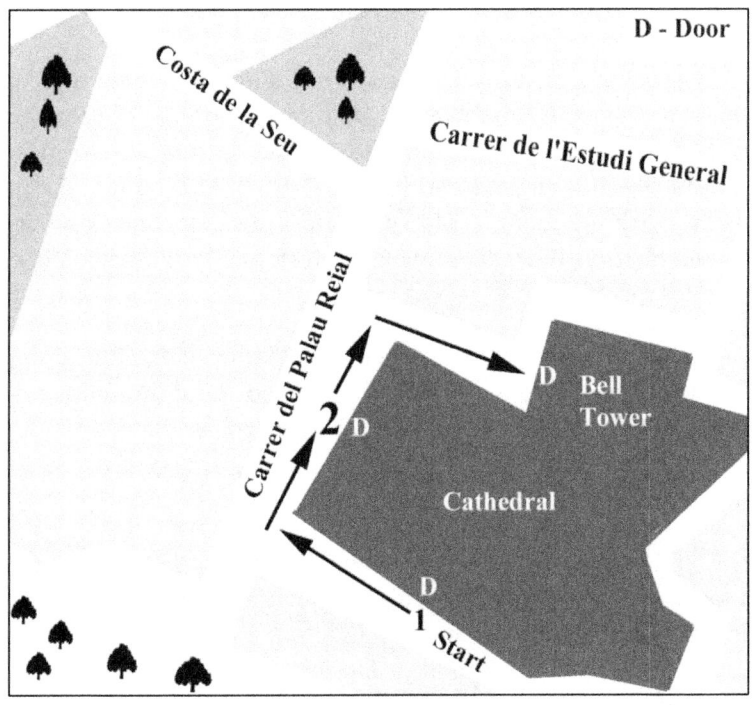

Map 1

Make your way to the Porta Del Mirador which is the huge door facing the sea.

Palma Cathedral

It is called The Cathedral of Light and it got that name for a very good reason. To see it you should try to get to the Cathedral door for opening time on a sunny day. You can check the times at

http://catedraldemallorca.org/en/

Take a few minutes to look around the outside of the Cathedral before venturing inside.

The Cathedral was built once the Christians had retaken Mallorca from the Moors in the thirteenth century. King Jaume I's armada sailed from Spain but ran into a terrible storm en route. The King prayed and promised to build a temple if God would only take them to Mallorca safely. As you know from the Potted History, they did survive that storm, and proceeded to conquer the Moors and retake Mallorca.

In thanks, King Jaume I started building this cathedral on top of the main Mosque which once stood here, to celebrate Christianity's victory over Islam. That does mean that if you pray in front of the altar, you will be facing Mecca, and not Jerusalem – oh well near enough!

The Cathedral took over four hundred years to complete, and it has been restored several times over the centuries. The last time was by the famous Spanish architect Gaudi. It's the second largest Cathedral in Spain after Seville and is considered one of the most magnificent in the world.

Porta Del Mirador

Since this doorway faces the sea, it has had to withstand more corrosion from the weather than the cathedral's other doors. It was restored in 2003.

It has many intricate carvings. Take a look at the Last Supper just above the door. As usual, John is at Christ's side and is taking a nap.

Above that scene sits God being worshipped by six angels. Below stand five saints, Paul, Andrew, Peter, John the Baptist, and James.

On the ground on either side of the door lie two stone cannonballs. They were catapulted over the city walls into the Moorish city when King Jaume's army laid siege to Palma during the conquest in the thirteenth century.

As usual the door used by tourists is not one of the Cathedral's grand doors.

Map 1.1 - Face the Porta Del Mirador and go round the left-hand side of the cathedral.

You will reach the Porta Major on your right, another intricately carved doorway.

Porta Major

Actually, this side of the cathedral collapsed in the nineteenth century after an earthquake, and the doorway is the only piece that survived. The wall around it had to be rebuilt.

If you look just above the doors, you will see an inscription.

Non Est Factum Tale Opus In Universis Regnis

There is nothing like it in any kingdom.

It's from the Book of Kings in the Bible and is describing the throne of King Solomon, but the architect obviously thought it described Palma's cathedral as well.

Above that stands the Virgin Mary surrounded by many religious symbols: a lily, a rose, the moon, the sun, a fountain, and many others.

Above the door is the largest Rose Window in the world — which you will be seeing in all its splendour shortly. Finally in front of the door is a circular mosaic which Gaudi added when he was renovating the Cathedral.

Map 1.2 - Go round one more corner to approach the door of the belltower.

When the Cathedral was built over the original mosque, it's said that the belltower was placed over the minaret. It is home to nine bells which are called:

N'Eloi
Na Bàrbara
N'Antònia
Sa Nova
Na Mitja
Na Tèrcia
Na Matines
Na Prima
Na Picarol

N'Eloi (Praise) is the biggest – it weighs about five tons, is over six feet in diameter, and was cast in the fourteenth century. It is only rung on very special occasions, such as the election of a new Pope.

The base of the belltower is where you can buy your ticket. Santiago Rusiñol wrote a book about Mallorca, and he wrote this about the cathedral you are about to enter.

> "On the outside you will see its armour,
> but enter and you will see its soul".

Walk through a few small rooms prior to entering the main body of the cathedral - you can browse around them later. For now, just march through them and enter the Cathedral. If you have picked a sunny day, you will be captivated by the light display.

The Rose Window

The Cathedral has the largest Gothic rose window in the world – it's a whacking fourteen meters across and is known as the Gothic Eye. It's positioned on the East side of the Cathedral to catch the morning sun, and the coloured glass throws a kaleidoscope of colour to the other side of the Cathedral.

It's also exactly positioned so that on 2 days, around the Winter Solstice, the reflection is perfect and a light image of the Gothic Eye lands just below the rose window on the opposite side of the Cathedral. Together they form a figure 8, which has symbolic meaning in Christianity – it's the union of the material and the spiritual world apparently.

The light from the Gothic Eye also shoots through the West Rose Window, and if you are outside looking at the west side of the Cathedral it will seem as if it is lit up inside.

Of course, none of this is by accident; the clever architects calculated exactly the orientation needed and where the windows should be placed.

You probably won't manage to visit on those specific days, but on any sunny day it's still a wondrous site. As time ticks by the reflection moves and traverses the Cathedral, lighting up the forest of columns as it goes.

Once you have taken enough snaps of the light show you can walk around the perimeter and have a look at the various chapels. You will get a little guide with your ticket which will help you identify which is which.

The pillars

Like most cathedrals there are lines of pillars holding up that lofty ceiling, but these pillars are exceptionally narrow. The advantage is a lightness and spaciousness, but the disadvantage is their fragility. More than once there have been collapses resulting in a rebuild of parts of the cathedral.

Chapel of Saint Sebastian

Mallorca was hit by the plague in the sixteenth century and the death count was terrible. Then a ship sailed in, on it was the Archdeacon of Rhodes carrying a relic of Saint Sebastian – one of his arm bones. The plague suddenly stopped, and the saint was proclaimed to be the patron saint of Mallorca.

So here he stands being pierced by arrows on the orders of Emperor Diocletian, who was infamous for murdering Christians and making saints. The relic which stopped the plague is in the cathedral museum which you will visit later.

On either side of Saint Sebastian stand the statues of Cabrit and Bassa. They were supporters of King Jaume II when King

Alfonso III of Aragon invaded Mallorca. King Alfonso was the nephew of King Jaume - but when did a family connection ever stop an invasion in the middles ages?

There was a siege in the town of Alaro in the mountains of Northern Mallorca. It seems Cabrit and Bassa traded insults with King Alfonso over the wall. Alfonso is similar to the word for fish in Catalan, so insults were thrown at Alfonso about his being a fish and best eaten with garlic. Cabrit means goat in Mallorcan, so Alfonso promised to grill him like a goat. Once the siege was lost, both Cabrit and Bassa were indeed roasted in public – and the Pope was so appalled he excommunicated King Alfonso.

The West Window

Above All Souls Chapel is the West Window, very much the supporting actor in the light show in the morning – but is itself still an outstanding piece of work. This was the most unstable part of the Cathedral, and it was damaged on more than one occasion by earthquake.

Chapel of Our Lady of the Crown of Thrones

The four angels in this chapel have wonderfully colourful wings and swirling clothes, and they guard the Virgin Mary. The feast of the Assumption (August 15th) commemorates the day Mary rose up to heaven, and as part of the festivities this entire ensemble is moved to the nave of the Cathedral.

Chapel of the Holy Sacrament

This will be the busiest chapel, as it's the most unusual and you will either love it or hate it.

You will find a modern redecoration of the chapel. It's a huge terracotta affair, with waves and seaweed built into the walls. It celebrates two stories from the bible, Jesus feeding the multitude with loaves and fishes, and turning water into wine. So, you see lots of loaves, fish, and wine.

Royal Chapel

Gaudi restored the Royal Chapel just last century. He replaced the altar with the alabaster altar you see now. He designed the extravagant baldachin which hangs over the chapel, and which represents Christ's Crown of Thorns.

The seats of the walnut choir are home to many intricately carved creatures, but unfortunately, they are off limits to visitors. Gaudi moved the choir from the centre of the Cathedral to either side of the Royal Chapel. This opened up the Cathedral so that you can now gaze right along its length, but it did put the choir out of reach for today's visitors.

The conservative priests and officials were frankly askance at some of the changes Gaudi put in place, so perhaps they heaved a very private sigh of relief when Gaudi died after a tragic traffic accident in Barcelona. His death is why that controversial baldachin is not actually the finished article; it seems it is a prototype which has been kept in place due to Gaudi's fame.

The Chapel of the Holy Trinity

You cannot actually see this chapel because it's behind the main altar which is off-limits. The tombs of Kings Jaume II and Jaume III are there.

The Chapel of Corpus Christi

The golden altarpiece in this chapel is another of the Cathedral's treasures. When the Cathedral was last renovated, the gravestone of the sculptor Jaume Blanquer was found beneath it.

It's worth spending a minute to look at the Last Supper which is in the centre. Which of the figures is Judas? It's the one at the end holding a bag of money. Again, John is taking a nap centre-stage.

The Cloisters

You will of course want to pop out to the cloister, but to be honest it's a bit disappointing after the glorious interior.

Once you have explored the Cathedral you could take a quick look around the rooms you whizzed through when you arrived.

Sacristy of the Vermells

This room is from the fourteenth century. It got its name from the vermillion colour of the cassocks worn by the choir boys who used to change in this room.

Centre-stage is the huge golden sixteenth century Monstrance which is named Custodia Mayor (Great Guard). It's actually made of silver and just coated in gold. A monstrance provides either a place to display holy relics or is where the priest places communion bread once it has been consecrated. When Palma celebrates Corpus Christi, this is one of the many religious items carried around the town.

Gothic Chapter House

The tomb of Gil Sancho Munoz stands in the middle of the room. He is better known as anti-pope Clement VIII.

An anti-pope wasn't an enemy of the church; in fact, an anti-pope had a serious claim to the position of Pope. The Catholic Church split during the Middle Ages resulting in up to three popes claiming the role at the same time. Clement VIII made his claim from Avignon in France until he was persuaded to stand down. As a reward he became the Bishop of Mallorca and reverted to his real name.

Baroque Chapter House

The highlight of this room is a piece of the cross Christ was crucified on – at least that is what is believed. It's housed in a very ornate and bejeweled cross which stands by itself in a little chapel.

Also spot the statue of Vincent Ferrer. He is raising a banner which is in Latin, but which translates as

> *Fear God and give Him honour*
> *because the hour of his judgment is come*

Remember the name Vincent Ferrer, as you will read more about him when you visit Santa Eulalia later on the walk.

Rather more gruesome is the arm of Saint Sebastian which can be seen through a hole in the golden reliquary. As mentioned earlier, it was this relic which was supposed to have lifted the plague from Mallorca.

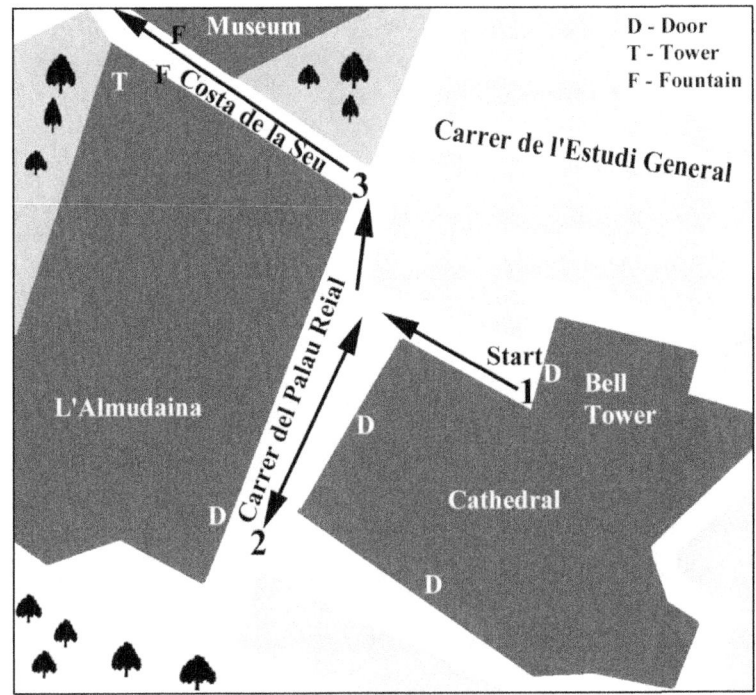

Map 2

Map 2.1 - When you exit the Cathedral, walk straight ahead and then turn left to return to the Porta Major which you passed earlier.

A little further along on your right-hand side is the entrance to L'Almudaina.

L'Almudaina

Originally the Muslim Alcazar stood here; a castle which was built soon after the Moors first arrived in Mallorca. After the Christian conquest it was turned into a Royal Palace and was modified by adding some Gothic features to it.

It has several mighty towers, and you can see two of them from this side before you go in. The largest of all the towers is called the Torre de l'Angel because of the bronze statue of the archangel Gabriel at the top – but you won't see it from this side of the building.

If you don't want to visit the palace, continue from "Leaving L'Almudaina" on page 23.

Otherwise enter and you will first reach the large courtyard which is where the soldiers marched and paraded. It now has palm trees and a little fountain.

On your left is the Great Hall. Inside you will explore a series of rooms, and as you do try to imagine the Great Hall as it was originally constructed. It was later divided into the two floors and multiple rooms you see now. The original roof of the Great Hall collapsed in the sixteenth century, and the king took the opportunity to split the vast room up.

Salo de Xemeneises

The Room of Chimneys gets its name from the three fireplaces which were originally used to heat the entire Great Hall.

Salo de Reis

The Room of Kings is home to nine portraits of Spanish Kings only painted last century.

Salo de Consells

This is the council chamber where a council was held by the King of Spain in 1983. If you look up to the arched ceiling, you can see a keystone decorated with the arms of King Philip of Spain. The room is decorated with tapestries which depict battles between the Spanish and the Turks.

Now climb up to the throne room.

Salo Mayor

The first thing that will strike you are the magnificent Gothic arches. This huge room is still used for Royal receptions, and it is decorated with many precious Flemish tapestries.

Arco del Mar

The Arco del Mar, Arcade of the sea, runs along the south side of the Great Hall and is where you can enjoy a lovely view over the Mediterranean.

Capella de Santa Ana

Go through the perfect arched doorway into a Gothic gem. The entire palace has been restored and altered over the years, but this chapel is the most authentic with little change. Find the Chapel of Santa Praxedes. King Jaume III brought relics of the saint from Rome and placed them in this lovely chapel where they are still kept today in a crystal urn.

Leaving L'Almudaina

Map 2.2 - With the palace door behind you, turn left to walk past the Porta Major once more. Keep going to pass both the Cathedral and L'Almudaina.

Map 2.3 - You will see a little garden on your left-hand side and a wide stairway leading down.

Behind the garden stands the *Bartolomé March* Foundation.

Bartolomé March Foundation

You could visit to see its collection of sculptures including works by Henry Moore, Barbara Hepworth, and Auguste Rodin. It also hosts an impressive library.

This was originally the home of the March family, headed by Juan March, a self-made millionaire. It was later turned into a museum by his son Bartolomé.

Continue by going down the steps on Costa de la Seu.

Costa de la Seu

You are now leaving 'high Palma' and entering 'low Palma'. As you do, take a look at the tower above you on the left.

Torre dels Caps

The original tower got its name (Tower of the Heads), because during Medieval Times the heads of the executed were hung from this tower as a warning to others.

However, that tower was demolished in the nineteenth century and its replacement was never used for such gory purposes.

Fountains

As you near the last set of steps, turn round to see two nice lionhead fountains.

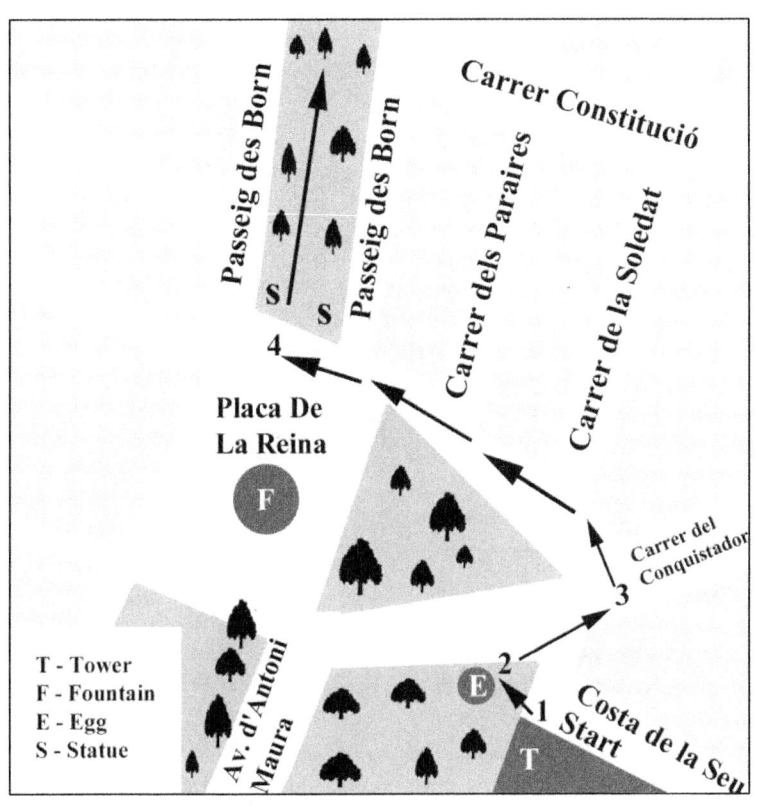

Map 3

Map 3.1 - At the bottom of the steps you will find Joan Miro's Egg.

Miro's Egg

Its official name is Monument a la Dona (Monument to the Woman), but its nickname is The Egg. It's made of bronze and was cast in 1972.

It's been likened to an egg sitting on top of a used bar of soap. Tourists love to stick their heads through the soap for a snap.

Miro came from Barcelona and was already famous when he settled in Palma, perhaps enjoying the anonymity he found there. Artists were not loved by Franco's Fascist government, so Miro wisely disappeared into the backstreets of Palma and lay low until the Civil War ended and a sort of normality started to return to Spain.

Palma remained unmoved by his art or fame, and it's said that Miro offered several sculptures to the city which were rejected. Now of course Miro is much loved by Palma and there are several pieces of his work scattered over Mallorca.

The Egg was bought by Palma council in 1978 and placed here - Miro himself chose this site for his creation. It was restored in the eighties when it was falling apart.

Map 3.2 - Stand facing uphill with the Egg directly behind you.

On your left you will see a large tree-filled traffic island. Beyond that you should be able to see or hear a large fountain which sits on the island.

With the Egg still behind you, walk straight ahead and uphill.

Map 3.3 - As you reach the start of Carrer del Conquistador, turn left to cross the road. Now walk downhill, always keeping the large tree-filled traffic-island on your left.

When you see the circular large fountain on your left, you will find the Passeig des Born on your right.

Sphinx

There are four stone sphinxes on Passeig des Born, two at either end. The locals call them the Lionesses of Born, but they are definitely sphinxes. In 1895 the council restored them and while they were at it, they reduced the size of their breasts by a couple of centimeters as they were thought far too provocative.

Passeig des Born

This street was once the bed of the Torrent sa Riera which often flooded and resulted in a lot of damage. It isn't a really a river, but in winter when the heavy rains pummeled Mallorca the water flowed down from the mountains and through Palma. The worst flood was in 1403 when the rains caused the Riera to flood and killed five thousand people. It took until the seventeenth century before the Torrent was finally diverted.

Map 3.4 - Walk up Passeig des Born under the shady plane trees.

You will reach a junction with wide Carrer Constitució on your right, and narrow Carrer de Sant Felieu on your left.

You may see various street artists and activities in the central reservation as you do.

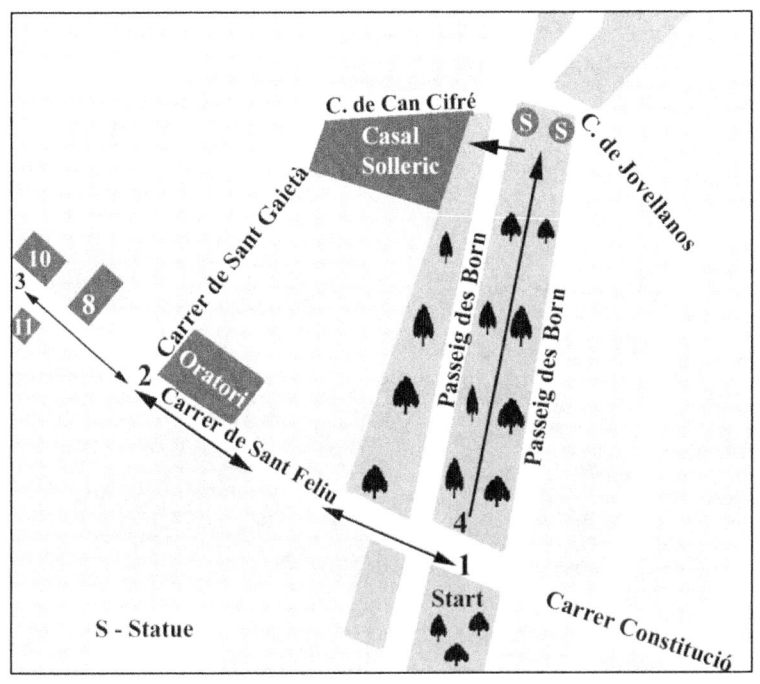

Map 4

Map 4.1 - If you have time, take a little diversion by turning left along Carrer de Sant Felieu. Otherwise, continue from "More Sphinxes" on Page 31.

You will find a little church on your right at the corner of Carrer de Sant Gaietà.

Oratori de Sant Feliu

This is one of the oldest churches in Palma, built in the 13th century after the Conquest. It has a lovely doorway with ornate carvings running across the top. The doorway is not quite as old as the church, as it replaced the original in the sixteenth century. There are also some ancient carvings just below the roofline.

If you are lucky the church will be open, as it is now a renowned art exhibition space. You can see the original Gothic columns and altar as an atmospheric backdrop to modern art.

Map 4.2 - Continue along Carrer de Sant Felieu to reach number 8 on your right.

This narrow little street is usually busy with shoppers. It is home to several interesting ornately decorated doorways like this one.

You will find the next one at number 11 on your left. Finally pause at number 10 on your right, Can Belloto.

Can Belloto

This doorway is topped with a huge face sticking its tongue out at you.

When the Belloto family bought this mansion, they had EUNDO carved above the face. It translates as LEAVING, meaning that everything we own is transient, no matter how wealthy we become.

Map 4.3 - Backtrack along Carrer de Sant Felieu to return to Passeig des Born. Turn left into Passeig des Born.

More Sphinxes

Map 4.4 - Continue walking up the avenue.

Make your way to the second set of sphinxes. On your left you will find the beautiful Casal Solleric.

Casal Solleric

The façade has a long balcony on the first floor, topped with five arches and lined with wrought-iron railings. Above the balcony you can see colourful decoration.

The Vallès family was one of Mallorca's oldest and richest families, and they were staunch allies and friends of the Spanish Royal family. King Charles III rewarded the head of the family with the title Marquis of Solleric. He announced that the honour was given in:

> *"recognition of the quality and splendour of your House and the services rendered by your Elders".*

Valles had the original buildings which stood here torn down and a sumptuous house built in their place. His architect was instructed to follow the Palma tradition of a beautiful courtyard with an impressive staircase, and to use the best materials available.

In 1872 Archduke Ludwig Salvator praised the courtyards:

"The patio of this house is one of the most beautiful in Palma, with a magnificent stairway passing under the segmental arches."

The house passed down the family line until 1975 when its last owners, the Morell family, decided it should be used for art exhibitions – which means of course you can go in and see it. At the time of writing there is an extra bonus – it's free!

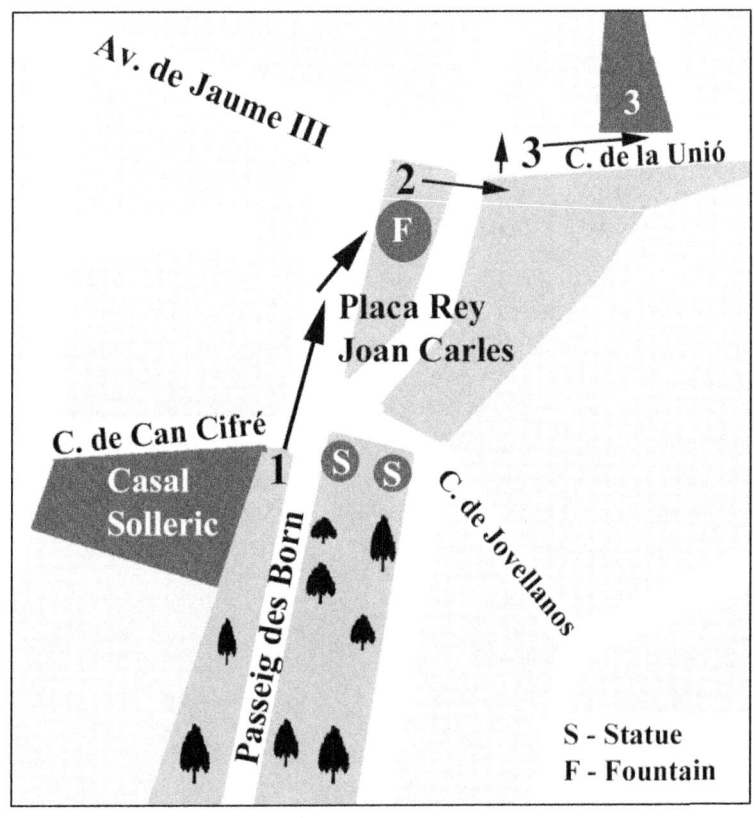

Map 5

Map 5.1 – With the door of Casal Solleric behind you, turn left to reach Plaça del Rei Joan Carles I.

Plaça del Rei Joan Carles I

This square is where the locals come to party on special occasions, for instance if the local football team, Real Mallorca, wins an important match.

The celebrations involve circling the fountain you see in the middle of the square, while beeping car horns and blowing whistles.

Make your way over to the fountain.

Font de les Tortugues

The fountain used to be called the Font de la Princesa in honour of the Princess of Asturias, who at just three years of age became Queen Isabel II de Borbón of Spain in the nineteenth century.

She clearly became less popular because in 1868 there was a revolution, and she was overthrown. This fountain was destroyed in the mayhem but was later rebuilt once peace and the throne had been restored.

The fountain hosts a rather bland obelisk, but there are interesting embellishments. At the top is a bronze bat! It's the heraldic symbol of Palma.

Look at the base and you will see that the column is being carried by four lovely tortoises and finally at the bottom are four lions dispensing the fountain's water.

Map 5.2 – With the fountain and the sphinxes behind you, turn right to walk into shady Carrer de la Unió. Use the pedestrian crossing to cross Carrer de la Unió.

The Torrent sa Riera ran along this street before turning down Passeig des Born. When it was finally diverted outside the old city walls, Palma's well-to-do started to build their houses here.

Map 5.3 – Turn right and walk along to number 3 on your left.

Here stands the Casal Balaguer - it's the one with the large wooden arched door.

Casal Balaguer

It is one of Palma's many patio houses which are built around a beautiful courtyard. It was built by the first Marquis of Requer, and the courtyard has the family coat of arms.

It has now been restored and reopened as another cultural centre, which means you can pop in and see the beautiful courtyard.

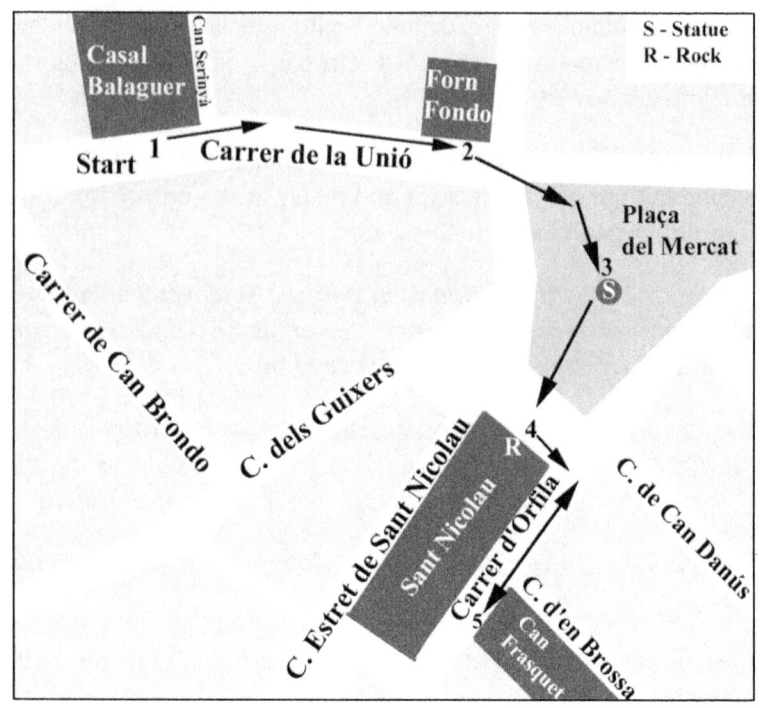

Map 6

Map 6.1 - When you leave, turn left to continue along Carrer de la Unio.

Pass Carrer de Can Serinyà on your left. Continue to number 15 on the left.

Forn Fondo

Here you will find Forn Fondo, a much-loved Modernist cake shop which might tempt you.

The bakery began business in the eighteenth century, when it stood by a bridge over the Torrent sa Riera which used to run along this street.

It was taken over by the Llull family at the start of the twentieth century. They completely renovated it and decorated it in the Modernist style you see now. Don't miss its beautiful corner streetlamp.

It's still owned by the same family and is famous for its ensaimadas – a sweet breakfast snack.

Map 6.2 - With the bakery door behind you, cross the street diagonally left to walk into Plaça del Marcat.

Make your way to the middle of the square.

Plaça del Mercat

In the middle of the square is the bronze Antonio Maura memorial. He was Prime Minister of Spain five times and came from Palma.

Beneath Maura stands Truth, which was his guiding principle. The bronze inscription says.

Antonio Maura, Igualó con la vida el pensamiento

Antonio Maura, He equated life with thought

Truth as you can see is dressed but she was originally supposed to be naked to represent "The whole truth". The draft sculpture caused a scandal, so the lady was quickly draped for modesty.

Of course when she was unveiled, critics interpreted it as saying that politicians only speak half-truths, which is probably closer to the mark.

Sant Nicolau Tower

From the square you can see the hexagonal tower of Sant Nicolau church behind the Antonio Maura memorial. It's the largest church in Mallorca. It was begun in the fourteenth century but rebuilt in the eighteenth.

Map 6.3 - Walk towards the church and find the Holy Rock attached to the church wall.

The Holy Rock

Catalina Tomas came from a humble family and was left an orphan. When she was old enough, she wanted to become a nun, but of course didn't have a dowry so the nunneries weren't too keen on her joining them.

While she waited for her local priest to find her a place, she prayed on this rock in the middle of Plaça del Mercat. When the good news came that she had a place, all the bells in Palma's convents rang out in celebration without anyone pulling them.

It's said that as a nun she was visited by devils and angels. She died in Palma and her body is preserved in a marble sarcophagus in the convent of St Mary Magdalene. She was regarded as a saint in Mallorca even when the Pope laid the law down and forbade the worship of unofficial saints. The people of Mallorca appealed and eventually The Vatican conceded, and she was made a saint in 1792.

In 1826 Palma wanted to rebuild this part of town, so the rock on which she had prayed was moved to its current location at the back of the church.

Map 6.4 - Now face the rock and walk down Carrer d'Orfila which is on the left-hand side of the church.

Stop when you reach Costa d'en Brossa on your left. Standing on the corner is Can Frasquet.

Can Frasquet

It's now a restaurant but until just a few years ago it was Palma's best sweet shop dating from the 18th century. It was owned by Josep Casasayas Casajuana – remember that name.

It was a much-loved landmark with an elegant façade and interior, with windows full of sweet temptations. You can see the original owner's name in an elegant engraving above the corner door. Sadly, the interior has been completely changed and modernised.

Map 6.5 - Now backtrack into Placa del Mercat once more.

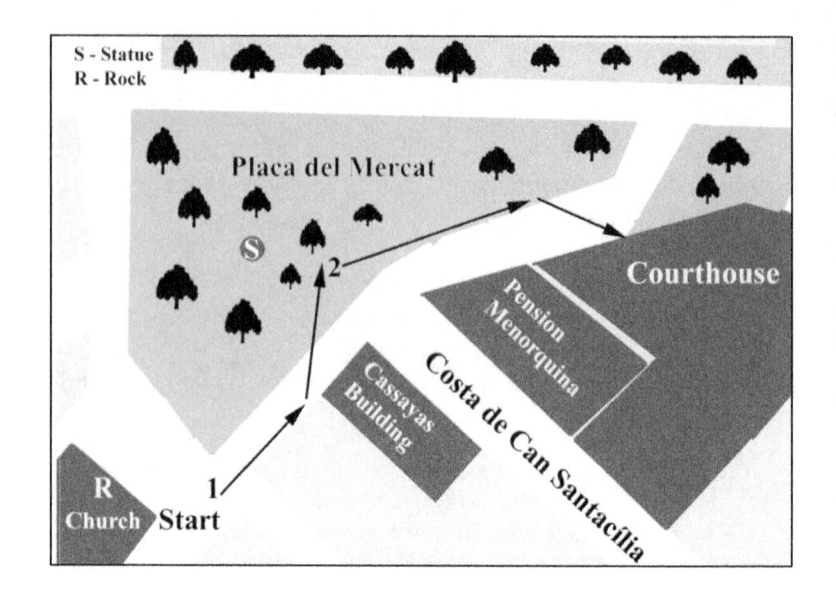

Map 7

Map 7.1 - Walk down the right-hand side of the square to reach the Casasayas building and the Pension Menorquina. They sit on either side of Costa de Can Santacilia.

Cross over into the square to get a good look at them.

Casasayas Building and Pension Menorquina.

These fantastic modernist buildings stand side by side and are split by a very narrow street. The term Modernist is notoriously difficult to pin down, but in the case of Catalan Modernism it's very like Art Nouveau with a bit of Gaudi thrown in. You can see that style clearly here with the design of the windows and doorways.

The buildings were commissioned by Josep Casasayas Casajuana, who owned the Can Frasquet sweet shop you just visited – there was obviously a lot of money to be made in confectionery.

You can see the initials of Josep Casasayas Casajuana on the façade of the right-hand building. It's at the very top on the right-hand side.

Map 7.2 - Now walk past both buildings and the next building on your right is the Courthouse.

Can Berga – now the Courthouse

This was originally a Moorish palace, but it was taken over by Augustine monks after the invasion, and later the Franciscan monks moved in. They didn't stay long as their church was built nearby, so this palace was sold to one of Palma's richest families.

In the seventeenth century it was bought by the Berga Family, and it's their coat of arms with the five crescent moons which you see over the door.

Finally, the Ministry of Justice bought it in 1950, restored and rebuilt it to the style you see today.

Originally the front door was on Costa de Can Santacília around the corner, as there was severe risk of flooding from the Torrent del Rei. Once the river had been safely diverted away, the palace was restyled, and the door moved to face the square.

If it's open, do go into the splendid courtyard for a look. It has an imperial stairway, that's one which splits into two giving you a choice of routes.

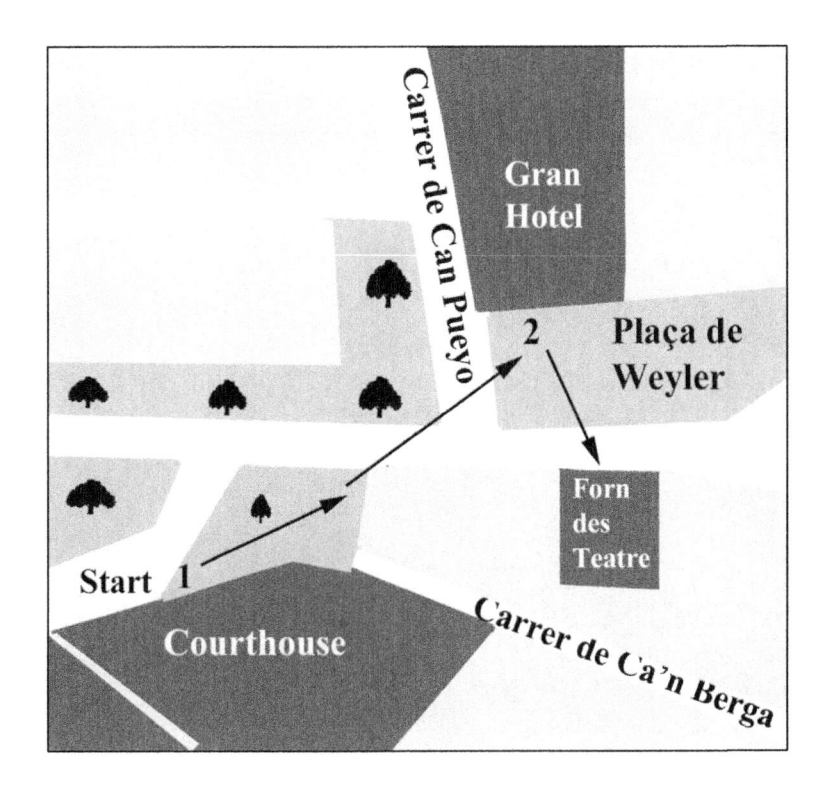

Map 8

Map 8.1 - With the main doorway of the courthouse behind you, look diagonally right to see the Gran hotel on the corner of Plaça de Weyler. Make your way over to it.

Gran Hotel

This was Palma's first modernist construction and was a sensation when built. It has an ornate façade sprinkled with ceramics, sculpture, and ironwork. As its name implies it started as a luxury hotel and was regarded as the most opulent hotel in Spain at the time. The Spanish author Miquel dels Sants Oliver described it in his book "La ciutat de mallorques".

> *"Waiters came and went, loaded with plates, silver sauce boats, sparkling crystal ware. Amongst the tables of the sumptuous dining room were scattered the many guests, some announced, others entirely mysterious, who came from the unknown to return to the anonymous, leaving no trace."*

Sadly, it had to close its doors as a hotel when the Spanish Civil War broke out. Mussolini sent a squadron of airmen to Mallorca to fight for Franco and helped him take the Balearic Islands early in the war. The Italian airmen were then billeted in this hotel and became known as the Balearic Falcons. They launched attacks from Mallorca to mainland Spain, and inflicted death and destruction on Barcelona and the rest of Catalonia.

After the war, the hotel became the National Welfare Institute and during their tenure the building was badly disfigured. However, since 1992 it has been faithfully restored. You will notice the lovely upper balcony at the corner - look up to see that it is supported by a circle of eagles.

At the time of writing, it is a culture centre. If you are interested it has a collection of Anglada Camarasa – a Spanish artist whose work is likened to Gustav Klimt. It's free so you could pop in.

You could also enjoy a coffee in the popular ground floor café while enjoying the view of the Casasayas building across the road.

Map 8.2 - With the Gran Hotel behind you, cross the road to reach the Forn des Teatre. It's probably hidden behind tables and sunshades.

Forn des Teatre

It was a pastry shop which opened in the nineteenth century. It closed for a time but has reopened and is selling delicious food once more.

Its ornate façade is listed. Look above the door. Some call the winged creature a bat, others a dragon, either way it has a rather impressive tongue. There is also an eagle above the window.

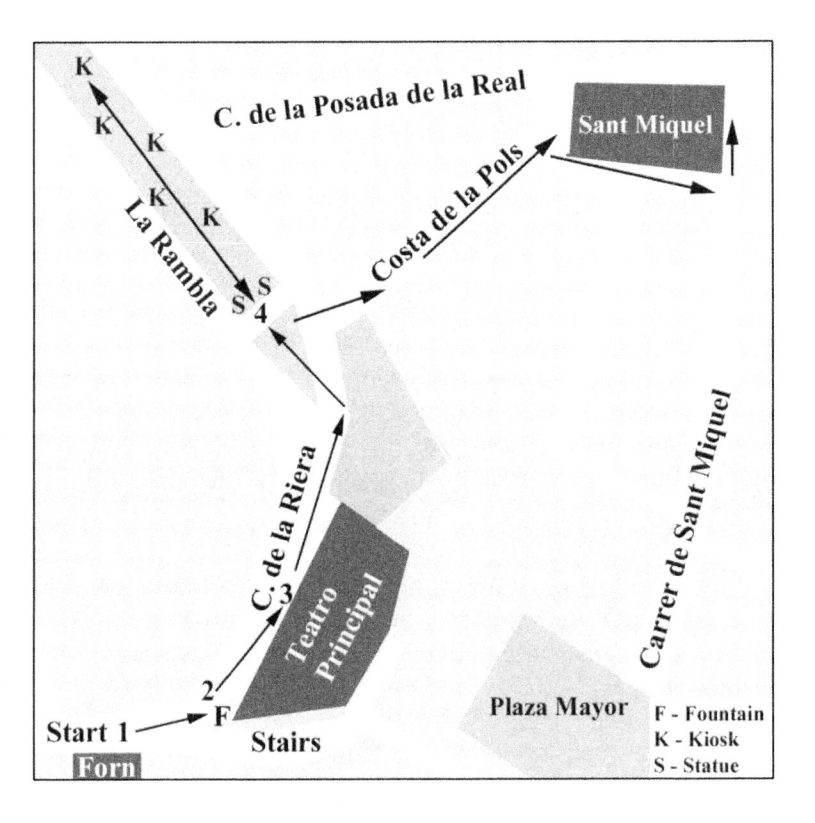

Map 9

Map 9.1 - Face the Forn des Teatre and turn left.

You will see a stairway leading up on your right, but don't go up it. Instead walk into Carrer de la Riera as it bends to the left. As you do, you will pass a little fountain called Nu.

Nu

It's a little fountain of a lady trying on a hat. It's a shame that at the time of writing it is not actually running, but perhaps when you explore you will hear the tinkle of water.

Map 9.2 - Continue along Carrer de la Riera to the front of the Teatro Principal.

Teatro Principal

As you face the building, look up and right at the top is a frieze full of mythological figures and the seven muses.

The first theatre was planned in the seventeenth century and was to be called the House of Comedies. Remember, those were times when the Catholic Church banned anything which was a bit of fun, and you were not really allowed to enjoy yourself. So, there was a debate amongst the theologians as to whether comedies were permitted at all. However, permission was finally granted, and the theatre was built and opened in 1667.

It hit a bad patch in the eighteenth century when it was used to house troops during one of Spain's many uprisings and wars. So once things had settled down it was replaced by a bigger and better building.

Disaster struck just one year later in 1858 when it burned down after a performance of Macbeth – the cursed play! Undaunted, the architects just rebuilt it again and it re-opened in 1860. It has since been renovated and restored to its former glory. It is beautiful inside, so if you like theatre you might be interested in what is showing.

https://www.teatreprincipal.com/en/

Map 9.3 - Facing the theatre, turn left to walk along its front.

Once past the theatre, continue to follow the road as it bends to the left. You will soon reach the start of La Rambla with its central pedestrianised walkway.

La Rambla

The Torrent sa Riera flowed down here in medieval times before turning into Plaça de Weyler. Disaster struck in 1403 when the river flooded, and an avalanche of water and trees broke through the city wall. It tore down bridges which crisscrossed the river and swept away the buildings in its path. Thousands died. The flood was called El Diluvi, The Deluge.

It took until the seventeenth century before the river was diverted to outside the town for safety; and this part of its old course became the Passeig de La Rambla.

When Franco finally won the Spanish Civil War, he renamed it Via Roma, as a thank you to Mussolini who helped Franco win the war. He also had the two Roman statues who guard the street put up to emphasize the point. The street was renamed at the end of last century, but the statues were left to celebrate Palma's Roman connection – and the locals call them "The Emperors".

This street is usually full of kiosks selling wonderful flowers. It's quite shady so it's a pleasant walk if you want to have a look at the flowers.

Map 9.4 - When you want to move on, return to the Roman Soldiers and face the same way as they do.

Turn left to go uphill on pedestrianised Costa de la Pols which has a number of little shops and cafes.

Map 9.5 - When you reach the top, you will see the back of a church and a set of steps on your right.

Climb the steps and follow the wall of the church to reach the front door of the church.

Sant Miquel

This was originally the site of a mosque, and according to legend this church was where the first mass was held in 1229 after the conquest. It was one of the first four churches built in Palma; the others are Santa Eulàlia, Sant Jaume, and Santa Creu.

It's been altered since then, but the stumpy belltower is the original from the thirteenth century.

If you look at the Gothic door you will see Ramon Llull standing on the left side holding a book.

Ramon Llull

He was from a wealthy family and became the tutor of King Jaime II. He was also a troubadour who liked to write love poems and really enjoyed life. Then out-of-the-blue he had a vision of Christ, not once but five times and it changed him profoundly.

He gave up the good life and dedicated his life to converting non-believers to Christianity – travelling all over Europe and North Africa to do so. He wrote about his visions in a poem.

When I was old and felt the world's vanity,
I began to do bad and entered into sin,
Forgetting glorious God, pursuing carnality;
But thanks to Jesus Christ for his great piety
Who revealed himself to me crucified five times,
So that I remember him and I fell in love with him

To help him convert non-Christians he devised "The Art", which was a debating tool. To answer any religious question, he followed the rules and charts of "The Art" to find the answer – which was always the Christian answer of course.

The really interesting thing though is that the charts and diagrams he used would be immediately recognizable to today's IT professionals, with trees, truth tables, and logical statements. It's claimed his system was the genesis of information technology.

He was also a prolific writer and wrote Blanquerna which was the first piece of literature in Catalan and perhaps the first European novel.

At the age of eighty-two he made one more trip to Tunisia to convert the Muslims, but it did not go well. He was stoned to death by the locals and taken back to Palma by some Italian merchants.

Inside Sant Miquel

Inside, first have a look at the main altar which is guarded by three of the archangels, Michael, Gabriel, and one of the lesser-known archangels, Raphael.

Each archangel is holding a traditional symbol, Michael the Warrior has armour and a sword, Gabriel the Messenger holds a flower (he gave one to the Virgin Mary when he broke the glad tidings of her unexpected pregnancy), and Raphael the Healer is holding a fish.

Virgen de la Salud

One of the very ornate side chapels on the right holds the statue of la Virgen de la Salud (Our Lady of Health).

When the King's fleet was hit by the storm on the way to Mallorca, the king desperately prayed to this statue of the Virgin Mary on his ship, and promised to build the Cathedral if his fleet didn't sink. As you know his fleet did survive and in thanks he placed the statue in this church. It later gained a reputation for healing, hence its name.

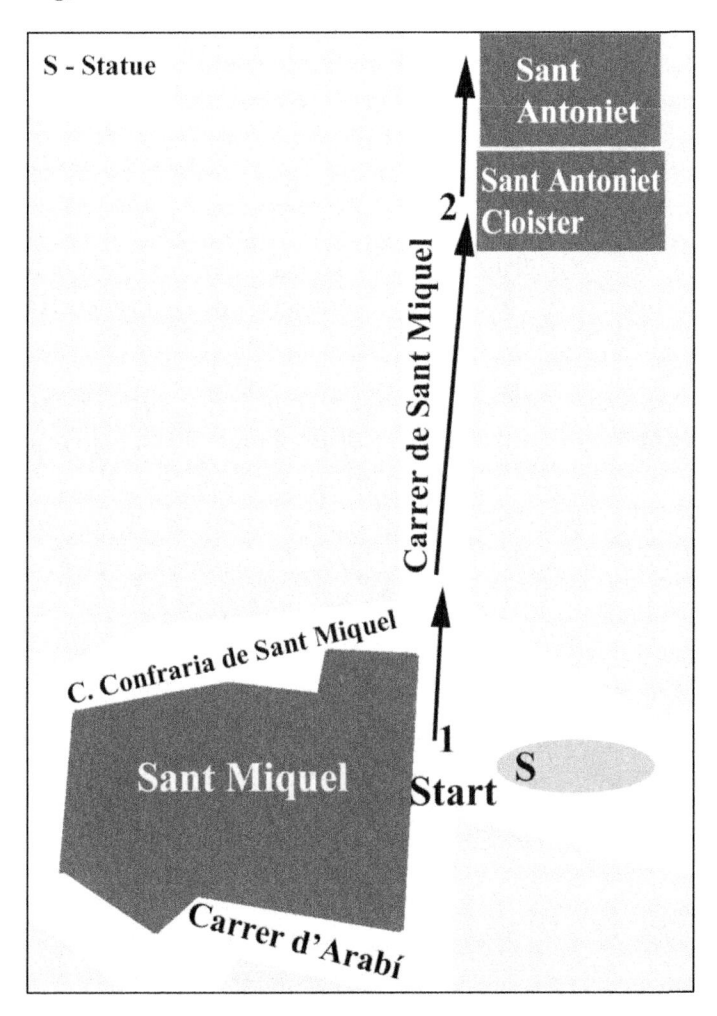

Map 10

Exit the church to stand in Plaça de la Mare de Déu de la Salut. Take a look at the little garden in front of you.

Pagesa

You will see a little statue called Pagesa. It's by Spanish sculptor Tomas Vila - as it states at the base of the statue.

The square you are standing in was renovated and Pagesa was removed for safety, but it was not returned once the work was complete. It only reappeared after a wonderful body called ARCA, "the Association for the Revitalization of Old Centers", asked the question of why it was missing and requested its return.

Map 10.1 - With the church door behind you, turn left to walk along Carrer de Sant Miquel. Stop at number 30 on your right.

Sant Antoniet Cloister

If the door is open pop in – it closes at lunchtime and at the weekend.

This is a gorgeous oval cloister which originally belonged to the church next door. However, the order of Saint Anthony was abolished in the eighteenth century, and the church and this cloister were given to the Sant Miquel church which you have just visited. The cloister is now owned by a bank and is sometimes used for art exhibitions.

Map 10.2 - With the door of the cloister behind you, turn right to reach Sant Antoni de Vana which sits next door.

Sant Antoniet de Vana

This is the church which originally owned the cloister. It's dedicated to Saint Anthony who stands above the door with a pig and a fire at his feet. He was a hermit who was repeatedly tempted by the devil but always rejected him.

Why is he shown with a pig? There are various legends. One tells us that Saint Anthony cured a dying piglet, another that he worked as a swineherd. Whatever the reason, since pigs were and still are particularly important to the island, his association with pigs is celebrated in all the villages. The local priest will station himself in the main square, and the townsfolk, dressed in their best outfits, drive their livestock past him for a blessing.

The fire represents St Anthony's fire, the old name for ergotism which is a particularly horrible disease – and which Saint Anthony cured more than once. The monks in this church were a hospital order and tried to help anyone suffering from the disease.

There are many devil dancing groups in Mallorca who celebrate Saint Anthony's triumph over the devil. Palma celebrates with devils wielding pitchforks and firework displays on January 16th/17th.

If it's open, pop in as it is a beautiful little church.

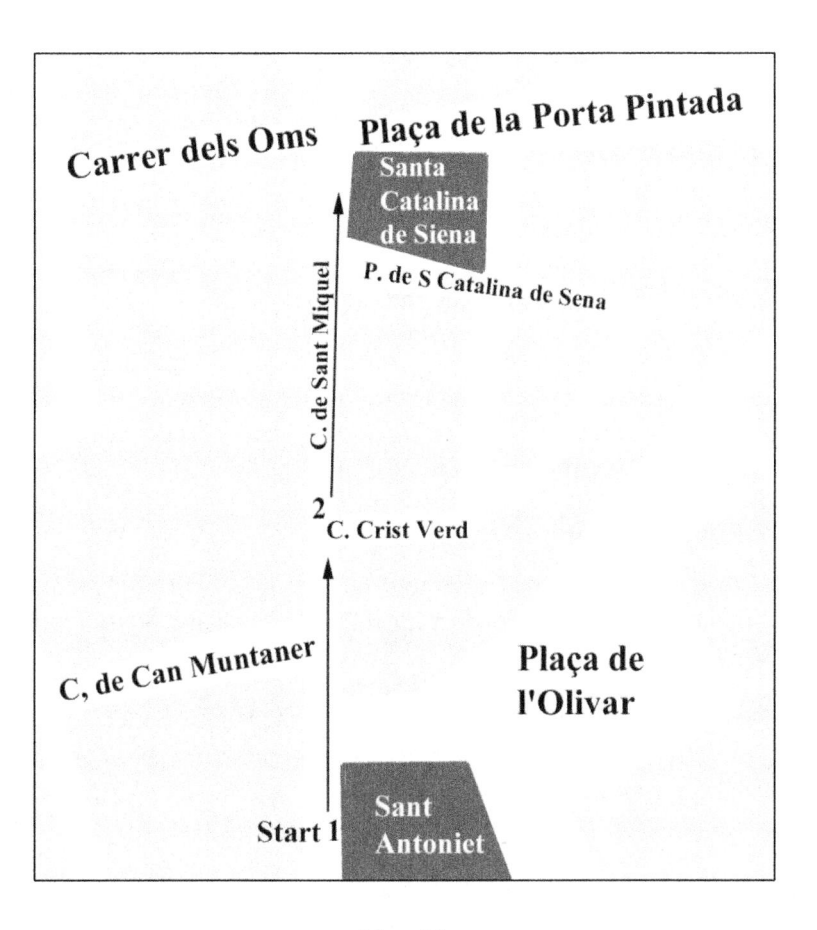

Map 11

Map 11.1 - With the door of Sant Antoniet behind you, turn right and continue along Carrer Sant Miquel.

Pass Plaça de l'Olivar and then tiny Carrer Crist Verd both on your right.

Map 11.2 - Continue straight ahead to find the Church of Santa Caterina de Sena on the right.

Santa Caterina de Sena

This church was dedicated to Santa Caterina of Siena. She travelled to France to persuade the Pope, who had taken residence up in Avignon, that the Catholic Church must return to Rome. Avignon was a much more comfortable and peaceful place to be, so she must have been very persuasive as Pope Gregory XI did finally up-sticks and return the church to Rome.

This church originally had a convent, but it disappeared long ago. These days it is used by the local Russian Orthodox community, and if you look at the opening times on the door you can see the days of the week in Russian.

Porta de Santa Margalida

You are very close now to the spot where King Jaume's Christian army finally broke through Palma's wall and poured into the city.

The Christian army fought its way down Carrer de Sant Miquel, while the Moors fought desperately to hold them back. The slaughter was horrendous on both sides, but finally the Moors were defeated.

King Jaume I entered the city through the Porta de Santa Margalida gate. Its older name was the Painted Door, Porta Pintada, which it got from the colourful crosses which were painted on the gate. It was demolished in 1908, despite many objections.

> EN ESTE LUGAR ESTABA
> LA PUERTA DE SANTA MARGARITA,
> POR DONDE ENTRARON EN LA CIUDAD
> D. JAIME E. EL CONQUISTADOR,
> Y SUS VICTORIOSAS HUESTES,
> DIA 31 DE DICIEMBRE DE 1229.

A plaque commemorating the battle, the entry of King Jaume, and the lost gate, can be found further along Carrer Sant Miquel.

If you want to see the plaque, cross over the junction beside the church. Continue along Carrer Sant Miquel until you reach Carrer Marie Curie on your right.

The plaque is on the wall of a modern building on your left. Make your way back to this church to continue this walk.

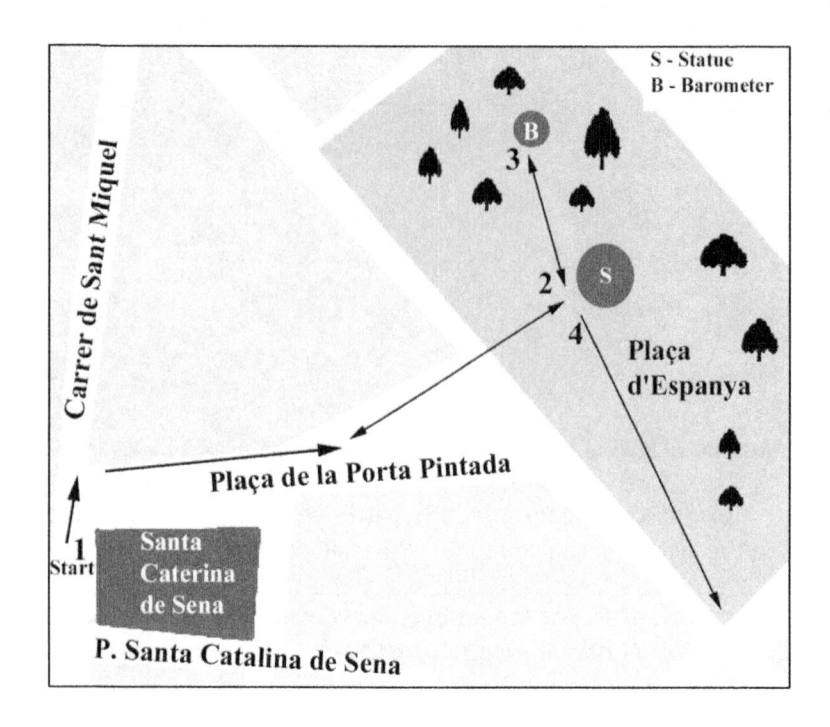

Map 12

***Map 12.1** - Face the church of Santa Caterina de Sena. Go round the left-hand side into Plaça de la Porta Pintada.*

Walk straight ahead passing the church on your right. You will walk into Plaça d'Espanya.

Plaça d'Espanya

This large square is the travel hub of Palma and if you are exploring Mallorca further you will probably catch a bus or train here. It's also where you can catch the old train to Soller in the mountains to the north - a lot of visitors visit Soller as a day trip. It's across the busy road in front of you and on the left.

However, the main reason for your visit right now is to see the impressive equestrian statue of King Jaume which stands in the middle of the square.

Jaume 1, Conqueridor de Mallorca

So, who was King Jaume I, the conqueror of Mallorca?

In medieval times Spain was not one country as we know it today. It was split into various kingdoms, and they were always battling or plotting to gain land, riches, or allies. The kingdom of Aragon was no different, but King Jaume finally decided that the Balearic Islands would be an easier and more profitable conquest than his neighbours. His Armada set off in September 1229 and as you know he eventually conquered Mallorca and the other Islands.

King Jaume had to eventually return to Aragon to ensure his kingdom remained intact. He had many children by his three wives and many mistresses, and when he died one of his legitimate sons became King Jaume II of Mallorca – he is buried in the Cathedral.

Not surprisingly the conquest of Mallorca by the Christian Armada has been celebrated in Palma since the thirteenth century. The festival is called the Festa de l'Estendart (the festival of the flag) and it takes place on 30th-31st December. There are various ceremonies and parades in Palma including the laying of flowers at this statue.

Map 12.2 - Now stand facing King Jaume. On the left-hand side of the statue amongst the trees is an intriguing relic of the past. Walk over to have a look at it.

Gaspar Bennazar Barometer

We are used to up-to-the-minute weather forecasts these days, but one hundred years ago the weather was much more of a mystery.

Gaspar Bennàzar was the chief architect of Palma and in 1910 he designed this beautiful old meteorological station. It's an ornate wooden column with dials giving various weather figures for temperature, pressure, and humidity.

Map 12.3 - Return to King Jaume and face the same way as he does.

Map 12.4 - Turn diagonally left and walk to reach the corner of the square.

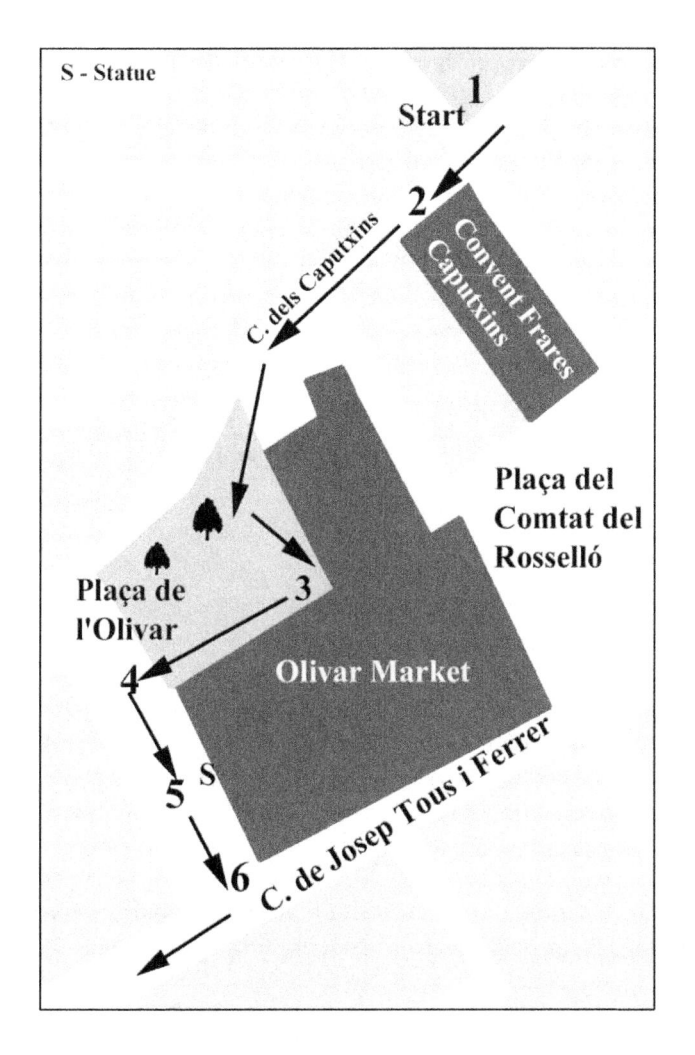

Map 13

***Map 13.1** - At the corner of the square, turn right into Carrer dels Caputxins.*

You will immediately reach the front of the Convent Frares Caputxins on your left.

Convent Frares Caputxins

This church still follows its guiding principle of helping the poor. Every morning, they open a side-door and distribute bocadillos (a filled baguette) to anyone who needs it. In recent years, the queue of hungry people has got longer, but the church soldiers on, trying to feed them all.

Map 13.2 - Walk past the church and along Carrer dels Caputxins. Walk into Plaça de l'Olivar, which fittingly is planted with olive trees.

Olivar Market

On your left is an orange building which is one of the largest covered markets in Europe.

Pop in and you will find stalls offering every sort of Spanish food you can imagine. There are lots of tapas bars, oyster stalls, and even sushi stands. So, if you need lunch, buy a selection of eats, sit down, and enjoy a rest. One very popular item is Serrano ham thinly sliced on crusty bread.

There are many exits from the market, so make sure you exit back onto Plaça de l'Olivar - the square you entered by.

Map 13.3 - Once outside, stand in the square with its pretty olive trees.

Have one wing of the market behind you, and the other one on your left. Walk straight ahead to reach the end of the square.

Map 13.4 - Turn left and walk along to a little set of steps on the left. You will see a statue by Tomas Vila sitting on the steps.

Tomas Vila

Vila was a Spanish sculptor. Palma has several of his statues on display - you have already seen one of them, Pagesa on Plaça de la Mare de Déu de la Salut. There are several others sprinkled around the island.

The statue shows us a very serious-looking old man with many facial wrinkles dressed in the traditional Mallorcan style – complete with the wide-legged trousers which are gathered under the knee and called calçons bufats.

Map 13.5 - Continue in the same direction to a T junction.

Map 13.6 - Turn right into a pedestrianised section of Carrer de Josep Tous i Ferrer.

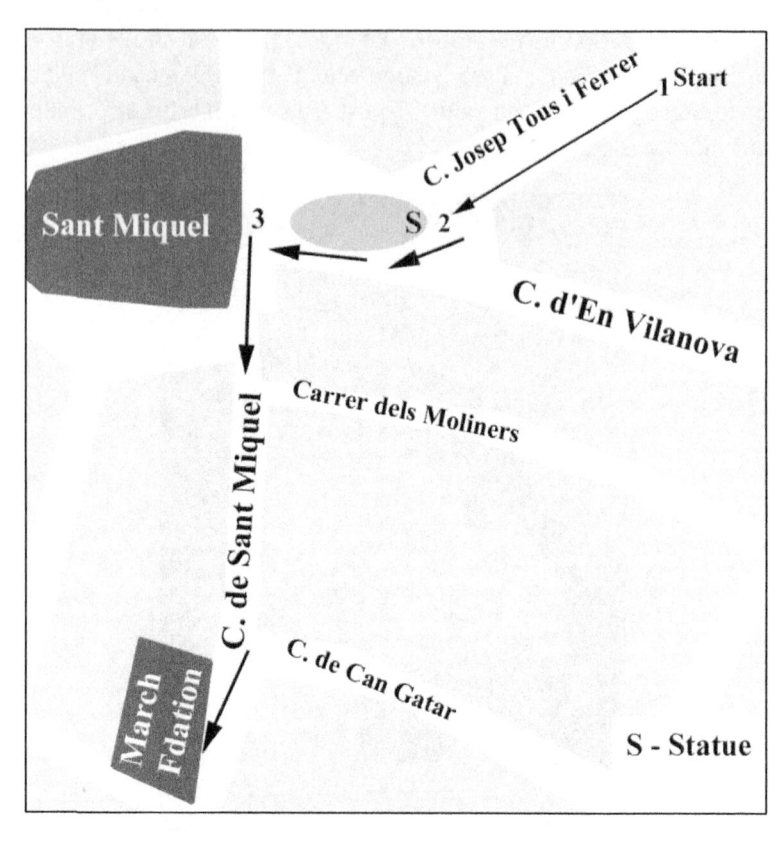

Map 14

Map 14.1 - Walk into Plaça de la Mare de Déu de la Salut which you passed through earlier.

Dona Cosint

At this end of the garden stands a rather blocky statue of a lady sewing, called "Dona Cosint".

The artist, Pere Pavia, was apparently inspired by the works of Sir Henry Moore. Pavia was awarded a medal from the Circle of Fine Arts in Palma for this statue, but it was then forgotten about and stashed in a warehouse. It was discovered years later in pieces, so Pavia recast it in bronze in 1982 and it has stood in this square since then.

Map 14.2 - Approach the door of the Sant Miquel church.

Map 14.3 - Turn left to leave the square on narrow but busy Carrer de Sant Miquel.

Pass Carrer dels Moliners and Carrer de Can Gatar on your left.

At number 11 on your right is the beautiful building which is home to the March Foundation.

March Foundation

This museum was built by local self-made millionaire Juan March to support the arts. That was his good side. On the other side he was a supporter of Franco; he helped him gain power and win the Spanish Civil War.

At the end of WWII, March was listed as one of the richest men in the world, and he accumulated one of the greatest private art collections which sadly is not on public view.

The museum is free to visit and is beautiful inside, so it's worth a quick look round even if you are not a fan of modern art.

There are paintings by the most famous modern Spanish artists, Picasso, Miro, Gris, and Dali, and a host of paintings by other less famous artists.

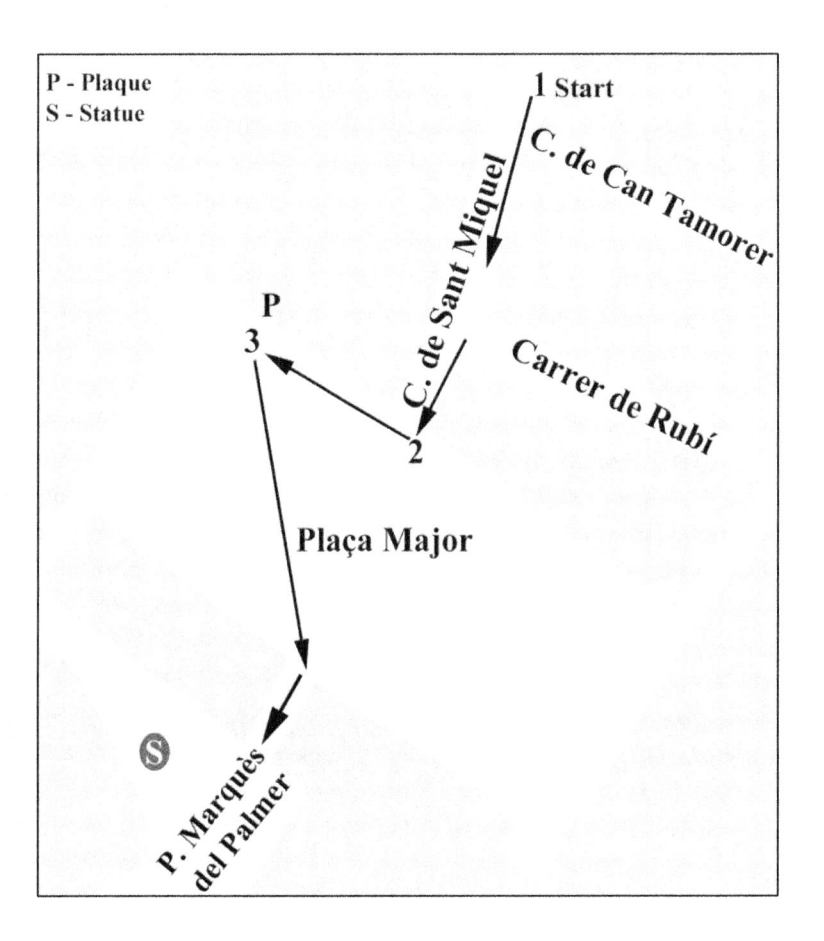

Map 15.1 - With the museum behind you, turn right to continue down Carrer de Sant Miquel.

Pass Carrer de Can Tamorer and Carrer de Rubi on your left.

You will walk into Plaça Major. Take note of which archway you entered by.

Plaça Major

This arcaded square with its traditional green shutters, is now free from traffic. It is full of street performers, bustling locals, and tourists armed with cameras.

Originally the San Felipe Neri convent stood here, but it was taken over to become the headquarters and torture chambers of the dreaded Spanish Inquisition. It was called the Casa Negra, the Black House, and it cast a frightening shadow over Palma.

It inflicted its ruthless dogma and horrific punishment on the people of Mallorca until 1823. In that year, the people sacked the building, burned all the documentation, and the Inquisition never returned. The prison bell was taken down and now sounds out the quarter-hour in Palma's Town Hall.

The buildings you see now were erected in the early nineteenth century. These days they are full of cafes and shops.

Map 15.2 - From the archway you entered the square by, turn right to walk along the side of the square.

Look above the arches to find the stone tablet which marks the birthplace of Ramon Llull.

Map 15.3 - Now exit the square via the archway directly opposite the one you entered by.

You will walk into another little square called Plaça del Marquès del Palmer.

Urbs

Spot what looks like two old Roman columns but is actually a piece of modern art called Urbs. Look closely to see the seashells, seahorses and starfish which decorate it. It was donated by the Rotary Club of Mallorca.

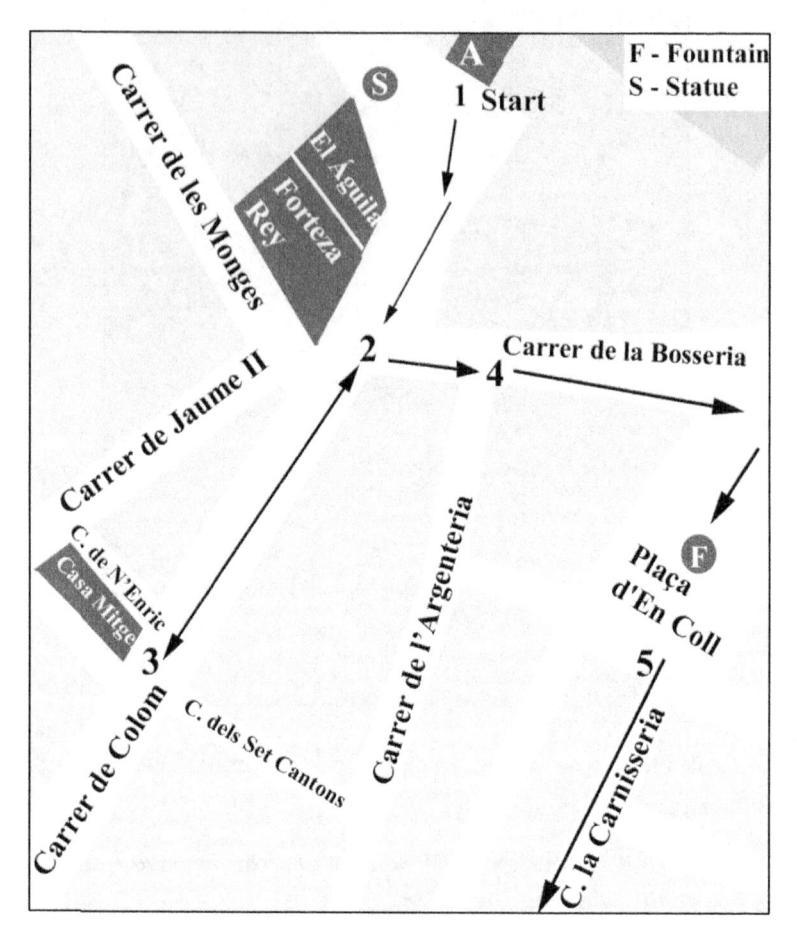

Map 16

Map 16.1 – With the archway behind you, walk across Plaça del Marquès del Palmer. You will reach Carrer de la Bosseria on your left.

On your right stand two wonderfully decorated buildings. Stand back to get a good view of them.

On the right is the El Águila building.

El Águila (The Eagle)

The building's name appears on its windows. The further up you look, the more ornate the decoration becomes with twirling iron balconies and stained-glass windows.

It was designed by Gaspar Bennassar who came from Palma – he was the one who designed the Barometer you saw in Plaça d'Espanya.

Just next door is the Forteza Rey building.

Forteza Rey building

This is another eye-catching building from 1920. It was the home of a goldsmith who befriended Gaudi when they were both working on the Cathedral.

You can clearly see Gaudi's influence with colourful roses, broken ceramic tiling, fruits, and flowers all built into the facade - and of course the demonic face which glowers at you from the first floor.

Two flying dragons flank the face. It's quite ironic that the grimacing face sits beneath the dentist.

Take a look at the corner of the Forteza Rey building on Carrer de les Monges.

Look right up to the top of the corner. You can just make out some sculpted letters – they spell out Rey – the owner's name.

Call Maior

This corner of the Forteza Rey building was at one time part of Palma's second Jewish quarter called the Call Maior. In the thirteenth century many of the wealthy Jewish families left the Jewish quarter which lay further south and built extravagant buildings in this area.

Map 16.2 - Stand facing the grimacing face on the Forteza Rey building. Turn left and you will see a fork in the road.

Go down the left-hand street, Carrer de Colom.

You will pass Carrer de N'Enric on your right and immediately after thar you will find the Casa de les Mitges.

Casa de les Mitges

Stand back and look up.

This building was inspired by the modernist Catalan architects of the day, especially when Gaudi arrived in Palma to work on the cathedral. You can see the varied materials used as you scan up the building, stone, tiles, and those curving mouldings loved by Gaudi.

It's finished off with eye-catching triangular balconies on the top floor. Beneath the triangular balconies you can see trencadis – a decorative collection of broken ceramic shards.

Don't miss the lovely floral decorations on both sides of the ground floor.

The building's name means "Sock House" and it got that name because the ground floor used to house a haberdashery – which presumably sold a lot of socks.

Map 16.3 - Now backtrack to the Forteza Ray building.

With the Forteza Rey's grimacing face behind you, walk straight ahead into Carrer de la Bosseria.

You will reach narrow Carrer de l'Argenteria on your right.

Carrer de l'Argenteria

You might have guessed that the name of the street comes from Argent, i.e., silver. This was part of the Jewish quarter and was where the silversmiths worked.

Map 16.4 - Continue along Carrer de la Bosseria to reach Plaça d'en Coll on your right. Walk into Plaça d'en Coll.

Plaça d'en Coll

This is another little square which is full of cafes and many colourful buildings, complete with a recently restored old fountain in the middle of the square.

ARCA have been battling with Town Hall for several years to try to restrict the number of tables and parasols filling the square.

So, if they have been successful, you might be able to see the fountain. If not, you will have to wend your way around the tables. Perhaps time for a refreshment?

Map 16.5 - There are two streets running south from the square. Take the left-hand street, Carrer de la Carnisseria (Butcher's Street).

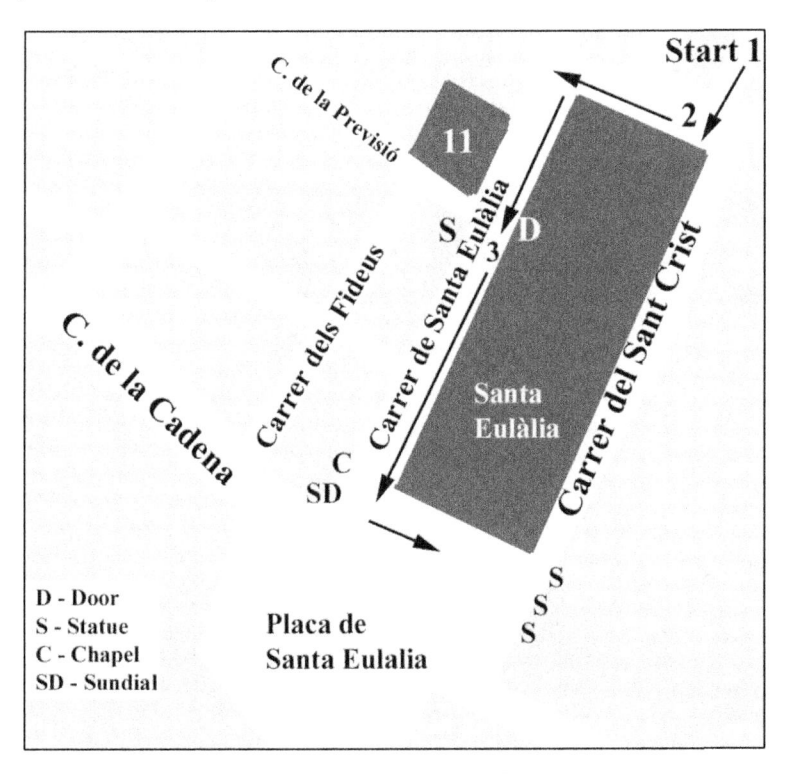

Map 17

Map 17.1 – Continue to reach the back of the Church of Santa Eulalia.

Map 17.2 - Go down the right-hand side of the church on Carrer de Santa Eulàlia.

Carrer de Santa Eulàlia

You will reach one of the main Church doors about halfway down the street.

Spot the sculpted figure of Jesus opposite on the corner of Carrer de la Previsió. Jesus does look like he is gripping his braces.

On the other corner at number 11 is a wine shop which specialises in Mallorcan wine, which might interest you.

Map 17.3 - Continue down Carrer de Santa Eulàlia and turn left to reach the front door of the church.

Santa Eulalia

The square you are now standing in used to be the church cemetery, then it became a market, and it is now full of tourists.

Santa Eulalia towers above you and is a large, elegant church. It was one of the first parish churches built after the Christian conquest and was where the first Grand Council held its meetings.

The church is named after a 13-year-old girl from Barcelona who the Romans tortured dreadfully before cutting off her head, all because she refused to recant her faith – her statue stands above the door.

Standing at the front of the church you might think it doesn't look that old, but that's because the tower and the façade were reconstructed after an earthquake in the nineteenth century. It has some good gargoyles looking down at you from above the door.

Until the late fourteenth century the Jewish and Christian communities in Palma had lived together in an uneasy alliance. However, Mallorca's Jewish quarter was attacked in 1391 as the Christians blamed them for any misfortune which befell the island. Many were killed or converted to save their lives.

The Jews did slowly return to Mallorca. Violence returned in 1435 and this time the Jews were offered a choice – convert or die. They mostly converted and it all took place here in Santa Eulalia – those who converted were nicknamed "conversos".

Officially there were no Jews left on Mallorca, but that wasn't enough for the Spanish Inquisition who arrived in 1478. They simply didn't believe the converts were really Christian, so accusation, torture, and burning at the stake for any suspects became common.

Go inside to see the huge rose window – it's not as big as the Cathedral's but is still impressive.

The pulpit was where The Angel of the Apocalypse, a.k.a. Vincent Ferrer, preached. You saw a statue of him in the

Cathedral earlier. He was a Fire and Brimstone preacher and travelled all over Europe to give his explosive sermons. He also produced a miracle or two, including stilling a storm when he was in Palma and wanted to preach to the locals. He was later promoted to a saint. There is a commemorative stone on the steps of the pulpit.

You can climb the tower for a great view over Palma. From there you can try to trace your route so far around town.

Plaça de Santa Eulalia

Once back outside, stand back from the church and look up to the top of the building to the left of the church.

Sundial

On the top balcony there is a sundial – you might have to use your zoom on your camera to see it. It shows a skeleton and a woman and under them is the cheerful phrase:

CADA HORA FER, SA DARRERA MATA

Every hour hurts, the last one kills

It's said that Mallorca has the highest concentration of sundials in the world. The island has over 800, and 112 of them are here in Palma.

Chapel

At the bottom of the same building on the Carrer de Santa Eulalia side is a tiny chapel. It's so small you won't spot it unless you know where to look. It's above and to the right of the shop window and there are usually some candles there. It was installed by the then owners of the shop.

Aurora, Meridies, and Vesper

Now look up to the second floor of the building to the right of the church. You will see three ladies who guard the square, Aurora, Meridies, and Vesper. They have been standing there since the middle of the last century.

Aurora with her open empty hand symbolises the dawn or the start of life, Meridies holds a fruit and represents midday and the middle of life, and Vesper with her closed hand represents night and the end of life.

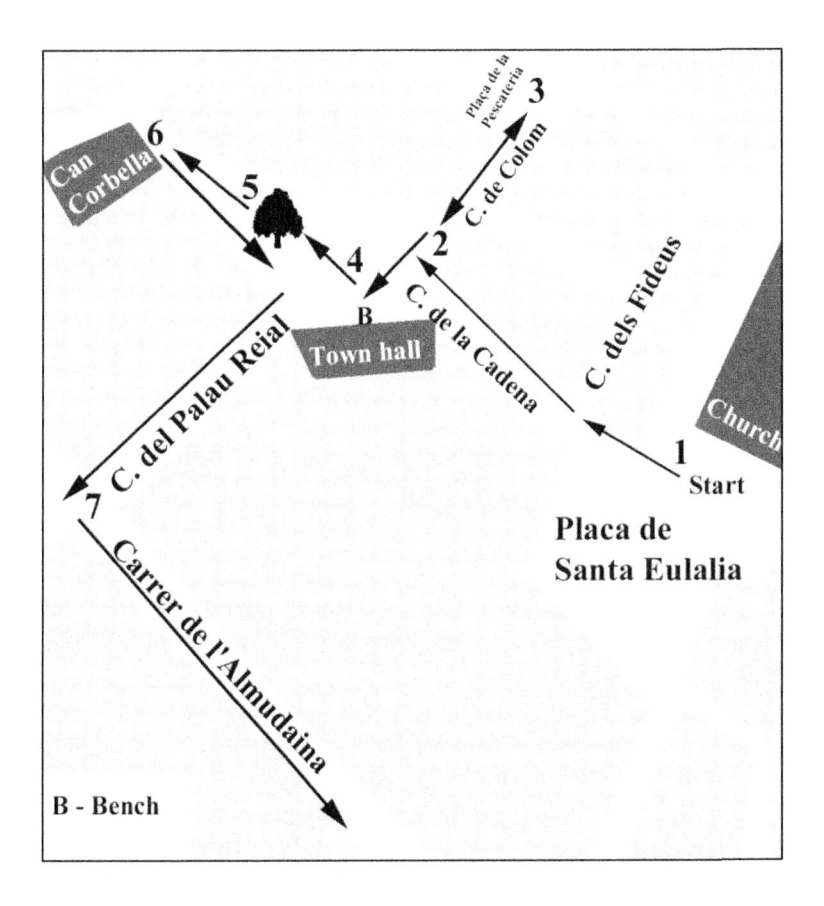

Map 18

Map 18.1 - With the church door behind you, turn right to leave the square by Carrer de la Cadena to reach Plaça de Cort.

Map 18.2 - Before exploring Plaça de Cort, turn right to walk along one block on Carrer de Colom.

On your left you will find Plaça de la Pescateria, fish square.

Plaça de la Pescateria

As you might expect, this little square was where the fish market was held as far back as the Middle Ages.

There are some shady trees and benches here now. In front of the benches, you can find Palma's stumbling stones. Unlike other installed stumbling stones found all over Europe, these little memorials have nothing to do with Nazi Germany and the holocaust. Instead, they remember the people who were murdered during Spain's fascist period.

Map 18.3 - With that sobering thought, backtrack along Carrer de Colom to Plaça de Cort.

Town hall

The impressive building with the flags outside is the Town hall – the site was originally a hospital, but the Town hall was built over it in the seventeenth century.

Spot the clock above the window, its nickname is En Figuera, and it's been telling the time for over 150 years. Like the rest of Spain, the way to celebrate the New Year is to pop a grape in your mouth on each chime of the clock. So, this is a busy square on New Year's night with people enjoying the party and ready with a bag of grapes as the New Year is rung in.

Today's clock is a standard 12-hour clock, but its predecessor had 14 hours. The reason was that in high summer there were 14 hours of sunshine and in winter 14 hours of darkness. So in summer, six o'clock in the morning would have been shown as hour 1 on the clock – very confusing. The clock you see now was bought from France and installed in 1863 when Palma decided to adopt the same time as the rest of Europe.

Outside is the bench of the "Sinofos" where you can sit down for a while. Local legend says the name comes from long ago when people with no intention of working for a living would sit here - the nickname Sinofo comes from the phrase "si no fos per" (if it wasn't for"). If asked why they weren't working, they would give what was thought a feeble excuse such as "if it wasn't for my sore arm".

Before you go in, take a close look at both sides of the left-hand door. About halfway up you can see two tiny sculptures of a lizard and a snail. They were put there by Jaume Caragol and Francesc Dragó who were stonemasons during the building's construction. Caragol means snail and Drago means lizard.

Earlier you read about the Festa de l'Estendart, Festival of the Flag. One of the ceremonies involves the laying of the Catalan flag here at the town hall.

Now step into the lovely foyer of the Town Hall. You might see the "gegants", huge mannequins which are paraded around the town during fiesta time. There are tours on Sundays at 11am but not in English at present.

Map 18.4 - Back outside on the square, walk over to take a look at the olive tree.

Olivo de Cort

The ancient olive tree on the square was placed here only in 1989. It was carefully transported from the Sierra de Tramuntana, the mountains to the north of the island. No one really knows how old the tree is, but it's popularly believed to have been planted the same year as King Jaime I arrived in Mallorca so that would make it over eight hundred years old! However, tree experts put it at 500 to 600 years old which is still pretty impressive. Amazingly it still produces olives.

People love to gaze at the ancient tree and try to spot patterns in the bark. Unfortunately, some thoughtless people have taken to climbing it just to pose for a photograph and have actually damaged the tree, so a fence has been placed around it for protection – such a shame.

Map 18.5 - Now walk past the olive tree to the end of the square. Find Can Corbella on the next left-hand corner.

Can Corbella

It's another ornate building but not strictly Modernist like others you have seen. Its style is called Neo-Moorish – those huge horseshoe arches on the ground floor are so similar to the old Moorish style which once filled Palma. The windows are filled with gorgeous stained glass.

If you stand back and look up, you can see a little octagonal tower.

The building got its name from a pharmacy which was on the ground floor, and which was called Droguería Corbella.

Map 18.6 - Now return towards the Town hall and take the first right onto Carrer del Palau Reial as you reach it.

You will reach a junction with tiny Carrer de l'Almudaina on your left and Carrer de la Victòria on your right.

Puerta de los Judíos

The gate to Palma's first Jewish quarter from Arab times stood where Carrer de la Victoria starts. Sadly, the gate did not survive the centuries.

The Jewish quarter was a small rectangular area from where you stand now down to the Almudaina fortress. The Jewish people lived there until the start of the thirteenth century when they began to move north into what was called the Call Maior.

Map 18.7 - Now turn left into Carrer de l'Almudaina, a wonderfully old winding street.

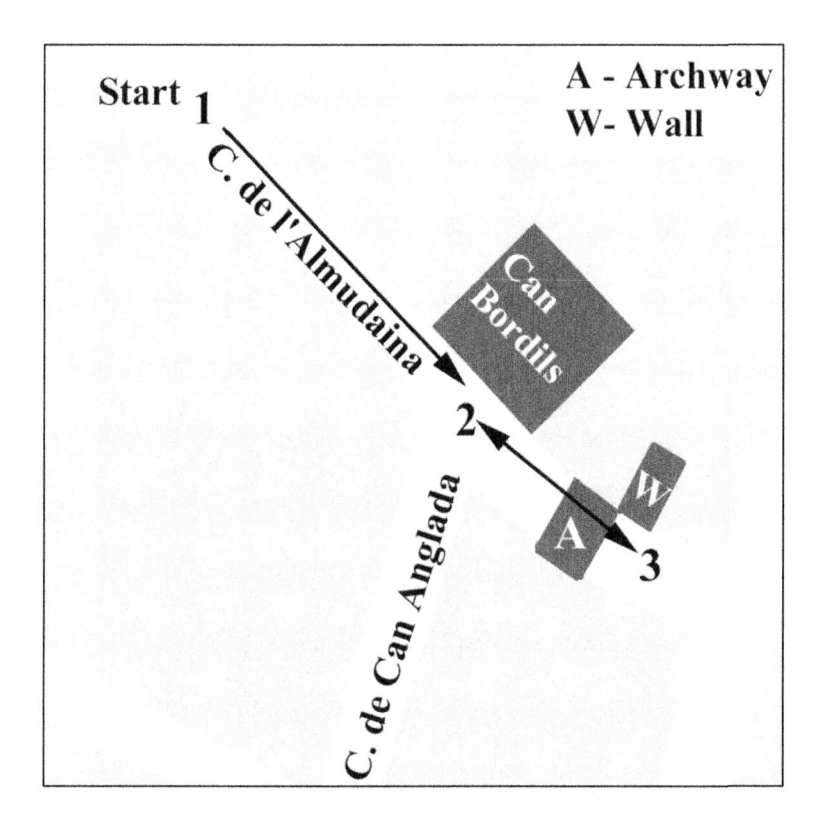

Map 19

Map 19.1 - Continue walking to pass Carrer de Can Anglada on your right.

Map 19.2 - You will see an archway in front of you, so walk down to have a look at it.

Arc de l'Almudaina

This arch is part of the old town wall from Arab times. Some historians think it's even older and is actually Roman.

Go through the archway and look left to see another piece of the old wall and an archway incorporated into the adjoining building.

When the Moors ruled in Mallorca, this gateway marked part of the boundary between the Almudaina where the rulers lived, and the Medina where the general population lived. If there was any sort of rebellion or trouble, the rulers just closed the gates to keep the rabble at bay.

Map 19.3 - Return along Carrer de l'Almudaina, passing under the archway once more. When you reach Carrer de Can Anglada on your left, you will find a building called Can Bordils on your right.

Can Bordils

This is now the municipal archive of Palma, so its gate is usually open letting you look round its beautiful courtyard.

It was built by the Sureda family, and it is their coat of arms which you can see above many of the windows, including two on the street. The building's name changed to Can Bordils when the inheriting daughter of the Sureda family married.

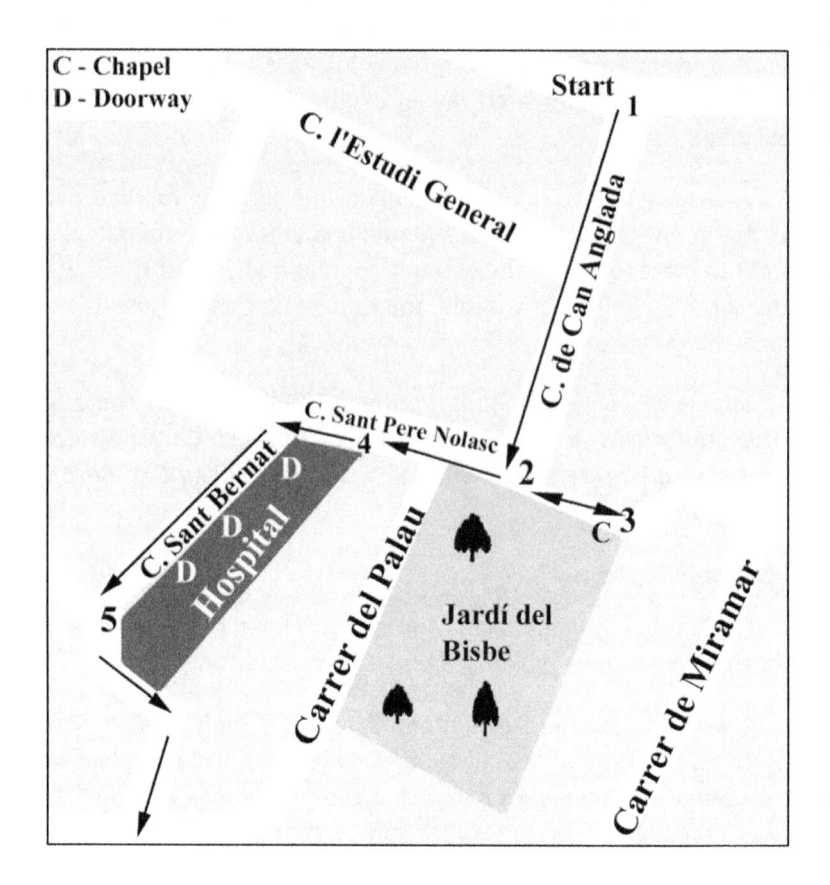

Map 20

***Map 20.1** - With the gateway of Can Bordils behind you, walk into Carrer de Can Anglada.*

Pass Carrer de l'Estudi General on your right and you will soon reach a T-junction and the entrance to Jardí del Bisbe.

Jardí del Bisbe

This botanical garden which belongs to the Bishopric of Mallorca gives you a chance to rest amidst a blast of refreshing greenery. It contains many native plants, fruits and vegetables and a pond filled with colourful goldfish and lilies.

Map 20.2 - When you are rested, leave the garden, and turn right a few steps.

You will see a little chapel niche which at the time of writing is decorated with plastic flowers! At one time it held a painting of the fire and brimstone priest San Vicente Ferrer. It was moved to a safer location and replaced with a wooden cross.

When the garden was renovated, the cross was removed, and probably sits in a box in the Town Hall somewhere. Perhaps when you visit, ARCA will have persuaded the authorities to return it.

Map 20.3 - Backtrack to pass the Garden entrance. Pass Carrer del Palau on your left.

Map 20.4 - Take the next left, Carrer de Sant Bernat.

As you enter this street You will see a large building on your left which has three very striking doorways. It is the Hospital de sant Pere i sant Bernat.

Hospital de sant Pere i sant Bernat

It was the hospital for poor priests, and it opened its doors in the fifteenth century.

The first doorway at number 1 is guarded by St Peter. The middle door has the Virgin Mary and Baby Jesus. Above them is a plaque commemorating the hospitals creation. The third doorway is guarded by Saint Bernard.

You can usually peep through the middle doorway to see the lovely courtyard.

Map 20.5 - Keep to the left-hand side of Carrer de Sant Bernat.

Wend your way down to a square where you can see the sea over the city wall.

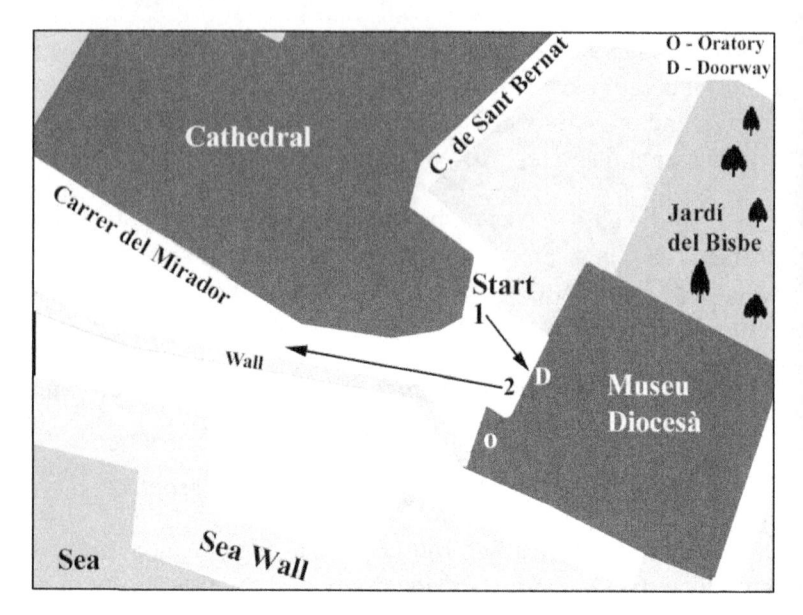

Map 21

Map 21.1 - On your left as you enter the square, is the handsome square doorway of the Museu Diocesà.

Just next to it is the beautiful arched doorway to the fifteenth century Oratory of Saint Paul.

Museu Diocesà

This is a beautiful thirteenth century building which is worth visiting for itself. You can wander under archways into little rooms which hold a museum of Christian art. You also get excellent views over the sea.

If you don't want to visit the museum, continue from "Leaving the Museum" on page 101.

The various paintings are accompanied by an English explanation of what they depict which always makes browsing more interesting. Here are some highlights:

George and the Dragon - Pedro Nisart

This is a colourful altarpiece of George and the Dragon with Palma in the background. It's thought that the artist based it on a lost Van Eyck. Beneath it are three more little paintings, and the last one shows the army of Jaime I entering Palma in 1229.

Santa Clara Altarpiece

The highlight though is an altarpiece which was taken from the Convent of Santa Clara. It shows us a series of paintings, each one depicting a key scene from The Passion. Find Palm Sunday and Saint Peter's kiss of betrayal.

On a less cultural and more curious note is the Drac de Na Coca.

Drac de Na Coca

This embalmed creature might look like a crocodile to you, but it is actually the terrifying Dragon da Coca.

It seems in the seventeenth century a dragon lurked in the sewers of Palma and hunted the streets at night. People reported missing pets and little piles of bones were found lying around. The legend grew as time passed and it was soon a monstrous creature which devoured children or old people. It was finally killed by Bartomeu Coch, embalmed, and now lies here for us to have a look at.

We can only guess that a Mallorcan trader or explorer brought it back from Africa and either let it loose or it escaped – and the poor creature survived the only way it knew how.

Leaving the Museum

Map 21.2 - With the door of the museum behind you, walk straight ahead along Carrer del Mirador with the sea on your left.

You can enjoy great views over the bay as you walk along the front of the Cathedral.

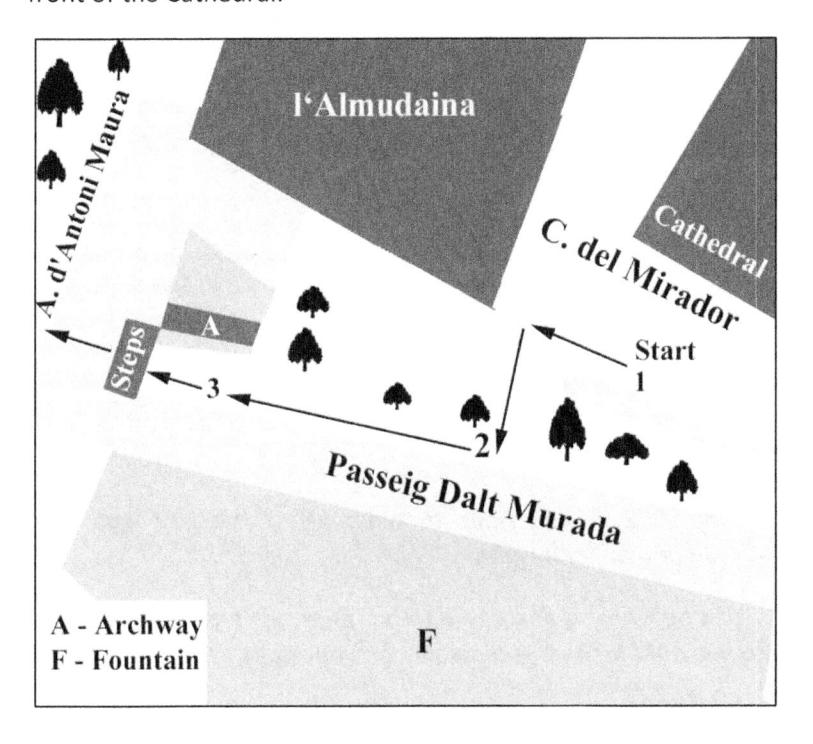

Map 22

Map 22.1 - When you reach the end of the Cathedral you will see the l'Almudaina in front of you.

Take the steps on the left down to the top of the city wall.

Miro's Wall

Walk to the wall and gaze across the little lake; you should be able to see a large colourful wall ceramic mural on the other side. It's another work by Miro. It's called "Wall for David Fernandez Miro" and is dedicated to his grandson.

If you are in Palma in the evening you should try to fit in a walk along that side of the lake. You will get wonderful views of the Cathedral all lit up and you can see Miro's mural properly.

Map 22.2 - Turn right to walk along the city wall with l'Almudaina on your right.

Just before you descend another flight of steps take a look at the huge old archway below you on your right.

Arc de la Drassana

This huge brick arch is 18 meters wide, and it is one of the rare Arab constructions to have survived the centuries.

It used to give access from the sea to a little port which was at the foot of L'Almudaina. There is a pool beneath it now, enjoyed by the local swans.

Map 22.3 - Now go down the steps. Cross a little garden to reach busy Avinguda d'Antoni Maura.

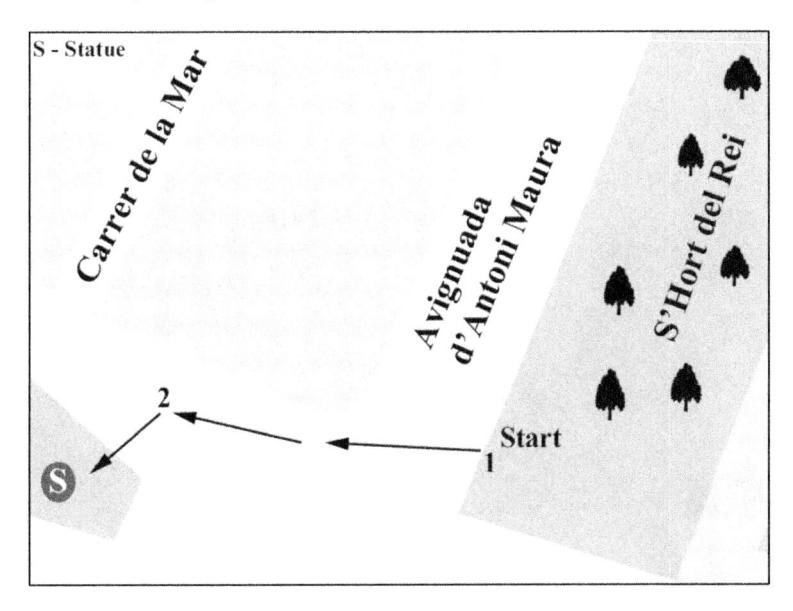

Map 23

Map 23.1 - Cross Avinguda d'Antoni Maura at the pedestrian crossing.

Map 23.2 - Once over, turn left and use another crossing to approach a statue of scholar Ramon Llull, who you read about earlier.

Lull is reading from a book. From here you get a glorious view of the cathedral.

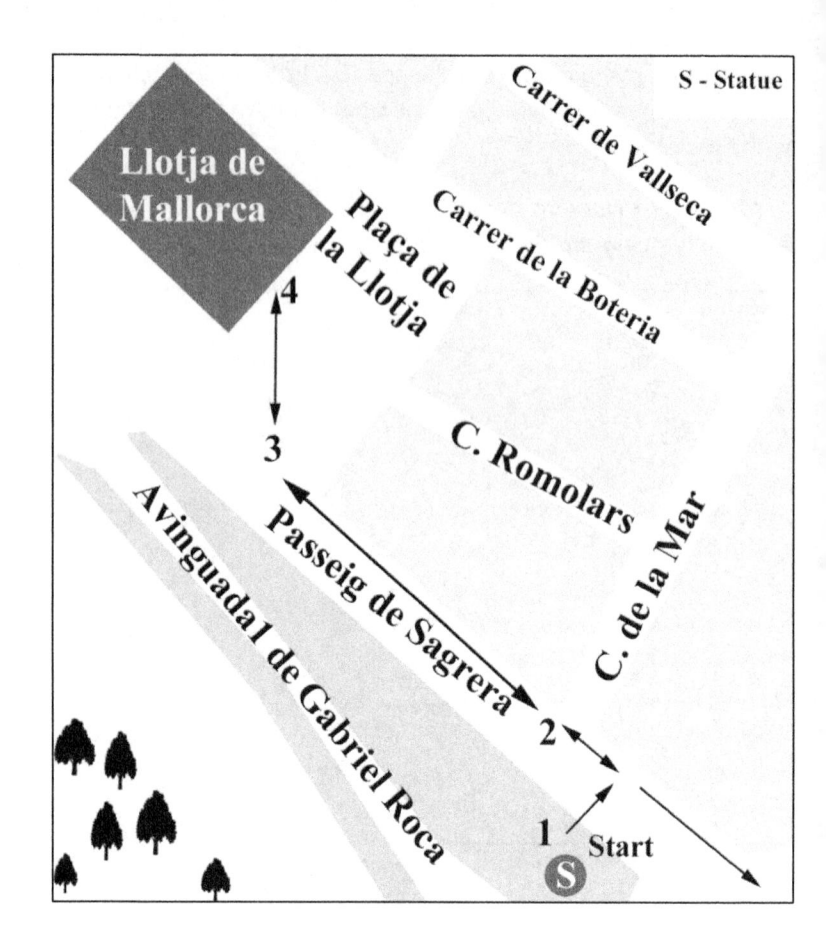

Map 24

Map 24.1 - Stand face to face with Llull. Turn left along the street directly behind him, Passeig de Sagrera.

Map 24.2 – Pass Carrer de la Mer then turn right into Plaça de la Llotja.

Here is another of Palma's highlights if you are a lover of beautiful architecture, Llotja de Mallorca.

Map 24.3 - Find the entrance on the left of the square.

Llotja de Mallorca

This was the maritime trade exchange built in the fifteenth century – designed by one of the greatest Mallorcan architects Guillem Sagrera who also worked on the Mirador Portal of the Cathedral.

It used to form part of the city wall. Above the door stands the Guardian Angel of Commerce – she is holding a ribbon with the caption:

Defensor de la Mercaderia

which means

Defender of Merchandise

Inside is a large hall held up by tall slim spiraling columns which look almost like palm trees. This was where the wealthy traders dressed in all their finery met and made deals.

Later the trade exchange was used for many less prestigious purposes including a prison, a hospital, and even a gunpowder factory. But finally, it was turned into a place for exhibiting the arts, which is still its purpose today. Even if you are not interested in art, go in to see the stunningly beautiful hall.

Map 24.4 - With the entrance behind you, cross the square diagonally right to return to Passeig de Sagrera.

Turn left and backtrack along Passeig de Sagrera, passing the statue of Lull on your right.

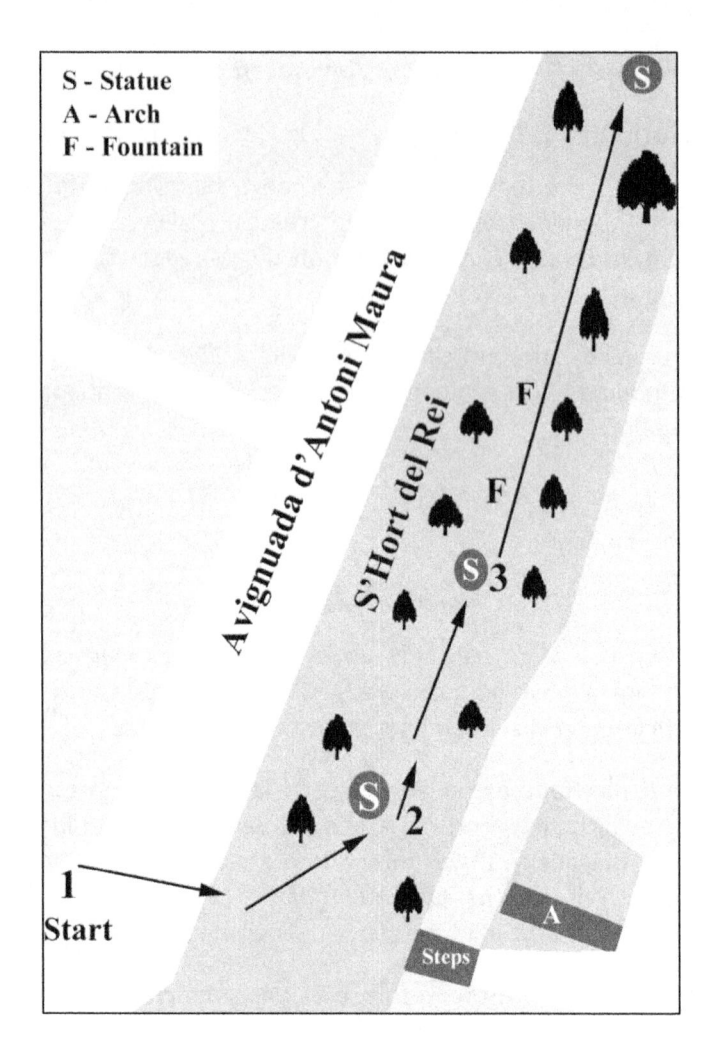

Map 25

Map 25.1 - Re-cross Avinguda d'Antoni Maura by the pedestrian crossing.

Turn left and you will enter the lovely S'Hort del Rei Garden.

S'Hort del Rei

This area was a walled garden in medieval times filled with fruit, veg, and flowers. They even bred rabbits here for the kitchens.

Over the centuries the walled garden disappeared under buildings of all sorts, but Palma's governors decided in the middle of the twentieth century to act. The garden was reclaimed from the real estate on top of it, and replanted to what you see today, with its fountains, statues, and shady trees. You might enjoy a rest here if it is very warm.

There are also some interesting statues sprinkled about. The first is Es Foner.

Es Foner

This wonderful bronze statue stands in front of some arches which give access to the little lake by the Arc de la Drassana.

It is a warrior using a sling to launch a stone at an enemy – Just like David felling Goliath in the Bible. The sling was a traditional hunting and fighting weapon long ago on the Balearic Islands. The skill of the Mallorcans in using it was mentioned by the Roman historian Livy.

The statue was cast by local boy Lorenzo Rossello who won a silver medal at the Paris Exposition in 1900. Rossello was greatly influenced by Rodin.

Map 25.2 – With the arches and little lake in front of you, turn left to walk through a gate and up the steps. Just in front of a fountain stands Jonica.

Jonica - Josep Maria Subirachs

Palma received this eye-catching marble sculpture as a gift from Subirachs in 1983. The artist is best known for his Passion Facade on the Sagrada Família in Barcelona.

This statue is an Ionic column which has been turned into a woman's body. Ionic columns have two scrolls decorating the top of the column, and in this case, they have become the woman's breasts.

On the base of the statue are some lines from a poem called Cançó de Jònia by the Greek poet Konstantinos Kavafis.

> *Although we destroyed their statues,*
> *even though we banished them from their temples,*
> *the gods did not die*

Map 25.3 – Walk past Jonica and the fountains to the far end of the garden to find Nancy.

Nancy

Nancy stands at the far end of the garden. This modern sculpture is perhaps a bit harder to appreciate than the others you have seen!

It's by Alexander Calder who was a friend of Joan Miró. It is actually a mobile sculpture; those antennae are supposed to move in the breeze. The original plan was to put it on the cathedral terrace overlooking the sea – where the sea breezes could work their magic. However, that didn't happen, so poor Nancy sits here motionless.

You have now reached the end of this walk.

Walk 2 – The Quieter Side of Palma

Walk 2 starts in Plaça de Santa Eulàlia, which you will have visited already on Walk 1.

It takes you to some lesser-known parts of Palma including what is left of the Jewish Quarter.

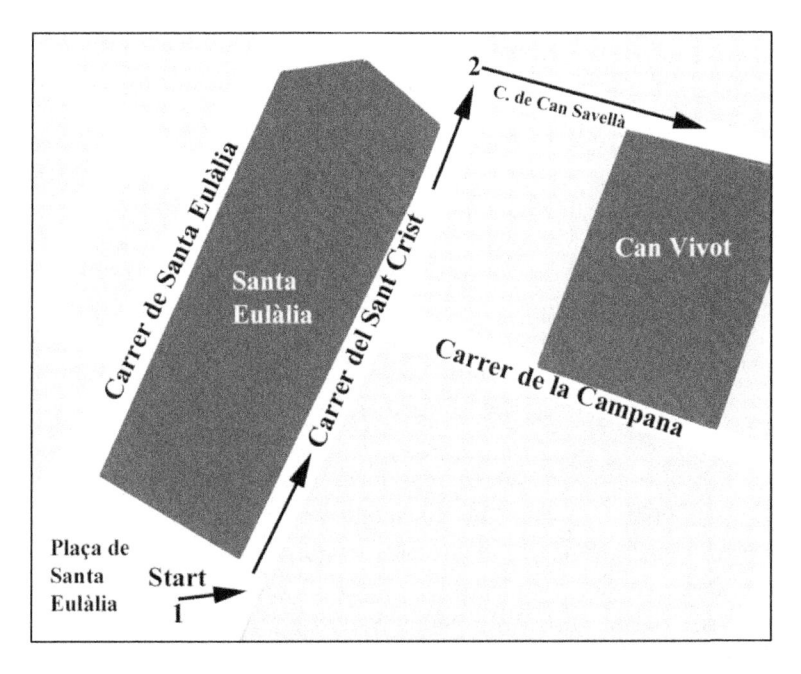

Map 1

Map 1.1 - Face the Santa Eulàlia church. Go round the right-hand side along Carrer del Sant Crist.

Map 1.2 - When you reach the end of the church, turn right into Carrer de Can Savellà.

This narrow little street lets you peep into some of Mallorca's beautiful traditional courtyards.

Pause at Can Vivot on your right at number 4.

Can Vivot

This house is usually open, letting you see the large courtyard with its arches and red marble columns. Even if the gate is closed you should still be able to see through the barred gateway.

The courtyard is cobbled and surrounded with impressive arches and another split imperial staircase. There are also some old carriages sheltering under the arches.

Archduke Ludwig Salvator of Austria visited in 1872 and declared that:

"The patio is splendid and should be counted amongst the most beautiful in Palma".

This house played a role in Spanish history. In the eighteenth-century Charles II, the King of Spain, was lying on his deathbed without a direct heir. He gave his kingdom to his grandnephew, the Duke of Anjou in France. Since Charles had ruled a huge empire, every European Royal house who shared any family connection made a claim to the throne and battles began.

The owner of this house was Joan Sureda and since he supported the French claim, plans were hatched in this house to support the French King. Once the battles were over, the French king rewarded Sureda with the title Marquis of Vivot. The house was renamed to celebrate.

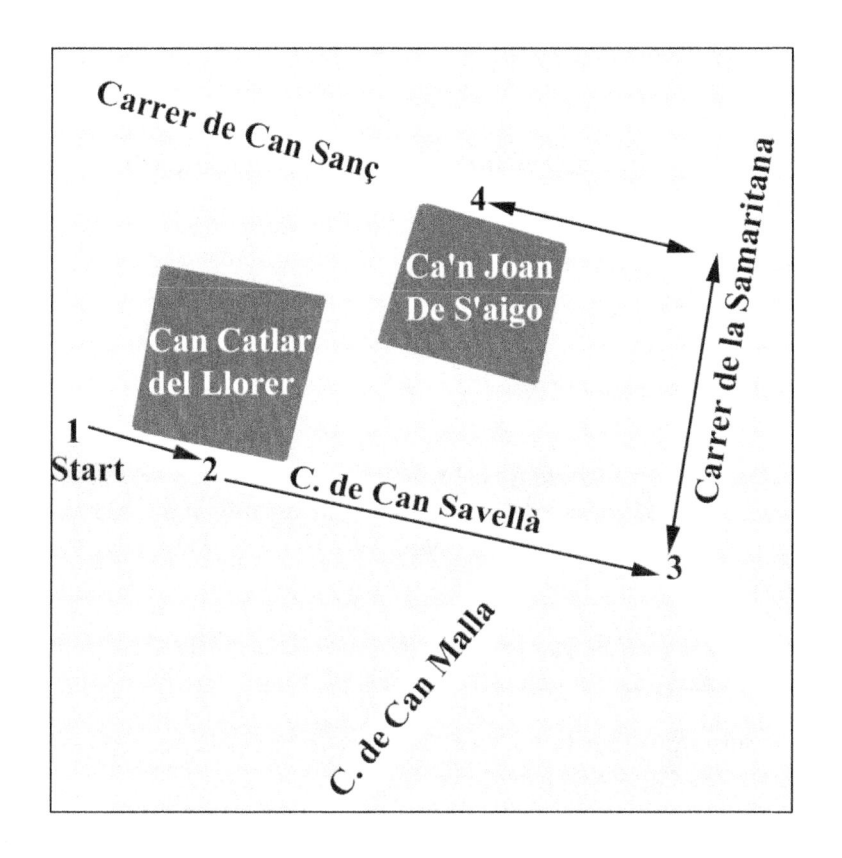

Map 2

Map 2.1 – Continue along Carrer de Can Savellà to number 15 on the left, Can Catlar del Llorer.

Can Catlar del Llorer

This one is not usually open, but you can peep through the gate to see its courtyard.

This is actually one of the oldest courtyards in Palma dating back to medieval times. When it was being renovated, the builders discovered some Gothic murals on the walls. They have been carefully preserved and if you visit the Museum of Mallorca later on this walk you can see them.

Map 2.2 – Continue to the end of Carrer de Can Savellà.

Map 2.3 – Turn left into Carrer de la Samaritana, and then left again into Carrer de Can Sanç.

You will find Can Joan De s'Aigo on your left at number 10.

Can Joan de s'Aigo

This café, which is worth visiting just for its lovely decoration, dates from the eighteenth century. It's a bonus that it also serves what are said to be the best ensaïmadas on the whole island – light as a feather and perfect with coffee. It's definitely worth a visit.

Map 2.4 - Now you are refueled, turn right out of the café to return along Carrer de Can Sanç.

Turn right to return down Carrer de la Samaritana. You will reach the T-junction with Carrer de Can Savellà.

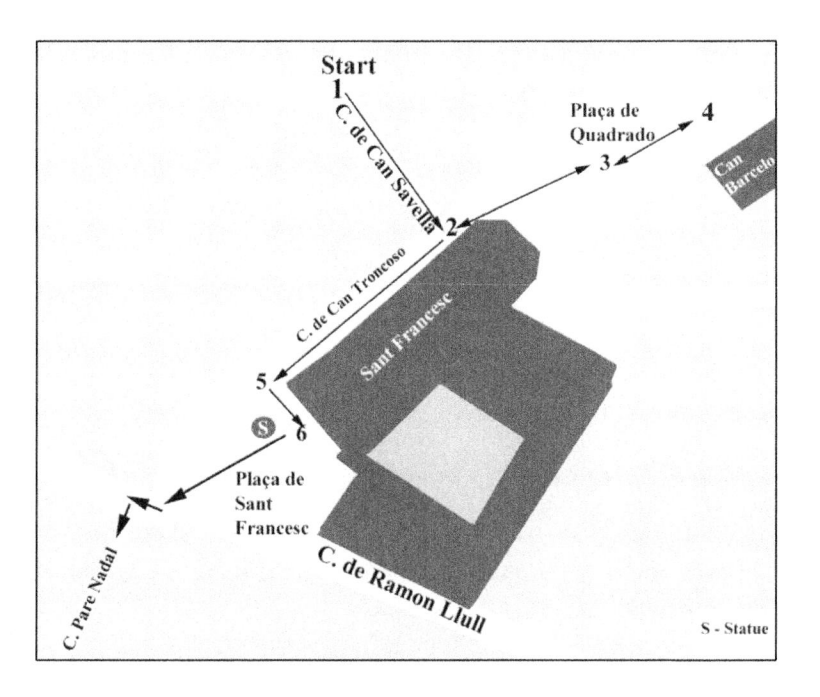

Map 3

Map 3.1 - Turn left and you will find yourself approaching the side of a church.

Map 3.2 - Turn left to walk into shady Plaça de Quadrado.

Plaça de Quadrado

This square has some handy stone benches under the trees for a rest if needed.

This square was where Palma's precious wheat was stored and guarded. When Mallorca had a bad harvest, the wheat was distributed to the people.

Map 3.3 - Walk past the shady garden. Turn right.

The building you see is another of Palma's modernist treasures, Can Barcelo.

Can Barcelo

You have to stand well back to see the lovely, tiled panels which run along the top between the wrought iron balconies. They represent architecture, literature, ceramics, music, industry, and trade, and are vividly coloured.

There are also some lovely blue butterflies in the centre panels above the balconies.

Map 3.4 - Now return through the garden to the back of the church.

Walk down the right-hand side of the church on Carrer de Can Troncoso.

Map 3.5 - Turn left to reach the front of the church.

Sant Francesc

This is another very old church which opened its ornate door in the early fourteenth century. Spot George and the Dragon above the main door. It's one of the most beautiful churches, and well worth a visit.

If you don't want to visit, skip to "Father Junipero Serra" on page 118.

The church got blasted by lightning in the sixteenth century which burned out the interior, and it took forty years to restore and redecorate it. They did it with style though, leaving a bright and inviting interior.

The golden altar has a revolving drum with each panel showing a different saint – including once again George and the Dragon.

Chapel of Our Lady of Consolation

The highlight of the church is the tomb of Ramon Llull who you read about in Plaça Major. His tomb is in this chapel and he is sculpted as though sleeping. He was beatified in 1988, which is the first step to being recognised as a Saint. You could drop a coin into the collection which is to help the campaign for his canonization.

Cloister

Go into the wonderful cloister sprinkled with orange and lemon trees and an old well. It's a nice spot for a breather. It should be peaceful but probably won't be because there is now a school on the first floor; so, don't be surprised to hear the sound of lots of children.

The style of the columns running around the cloister illustrates how long it took to build. The oldest are quite simple from the thirteenth century, and the most elaborate are from the fifteenth century.

Father Junipero Serra

Father Serra stands outside the church with a native North American child. He was Mallorca's most famous missionary.

He taught here at the Sant Francesc convent but then set out west for the New World. He started many missions in California, which turned into many of the state's best-known cities, including Los Angeles, and of course San Francisco.

Map 3.6 - Stand facing away from the front of the church. Cross the square diagonally right to leave the square.

Turn right along Carrer de Sant Francesc. After just a few steps turn left along Carrer del Pare Nadal.

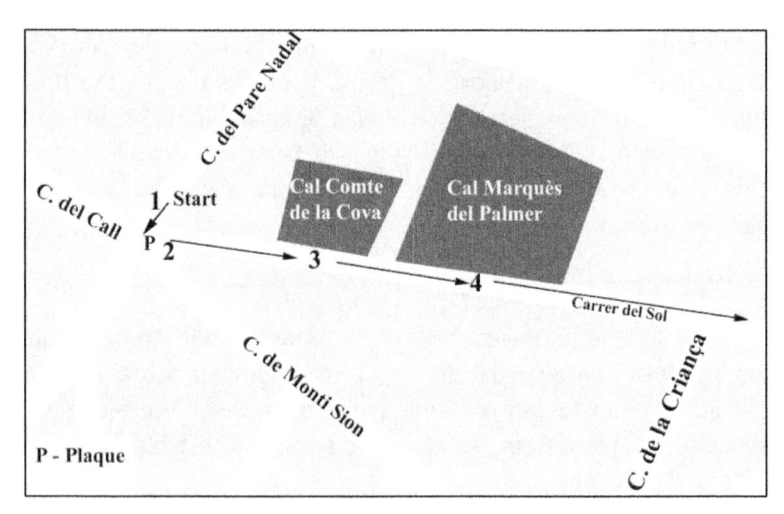

Map 4

Map 4.1 - Walk down Carrer del Pare Nadal to reach a five-way junction.

Sefarad symbol

The Gate of the Jews once stood here, the main entrance to the Jewish quarter. It's commemorated with a golden Sefarad symbol which you will find on a cobblestone in the middle of the junction. Sefarad is the Hebrew name for the Iberian Peninsula of Portugal and Spain.

Map 4.2 – Turn sharply left to leave the junction by Carrer del Sol. Walk along to number 4 on your right. Opposite it is the gateway to the Cal Comte de la Cova.

Cal Comte de la Cova

This building is built around another lovely courtyard, and since this medieval house is now the Faculty of Tourism, the gate should be open. You can admire its handsome staircase and its painted wooden roof.

Map 4.3 - A little further along you will find number 7 on your left.

Cal Marquès del Palmer

The original building which stood here in the fifteenth century was la Seca, the Mallorcan mint. It was later renovated and gained the beautiful facade you see now.

Take a look at the window on the left-hand side of the door. Above the window you see two angels holding the coat of arms of the Descatlar family. The title of Keeper of the Mint was given to Pere Abrí-Descatlar y de Santacoloma by King Alfonso V

The other window on the right-hand side shows us a woman stabbing herself in the breast with a sword. The experts think she represents Lucretia of Roman legend. She was raped by a prince of Rome when Rome was stilled ruled by a king. Once her father and husband swore to avenge her, she stabbed herself to death. Her family then led a rebellion which ended the rule of the king and led to Rome becoming a republic.

Map 4.4 - Continue along Carrer del Sol, passing Carrer de la Criança on you right.

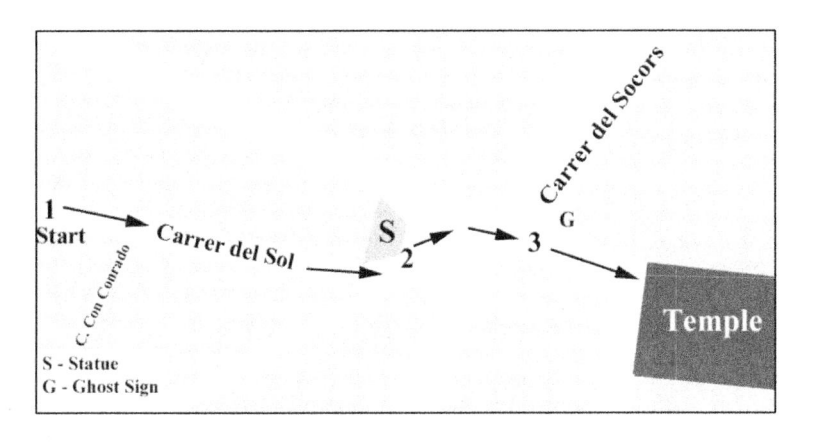

```
             1
         Start    Carrer del Sol    S   →  → 3    G
                                       2
         S - Statue
         G - Ghost Sign                                Temple
```

Map 5

Map 5.1 – Continue, passing and Carrer Con Conrado on you right and you will reach another junction. You will find a little triangular garden on your left.

You are now in the old Jewish quarter. If you remember from the Potted History, the Jewish quarter moved three times in Palma's history, and this is its third and final site, the Call Major.

Jafuda Cresques

A statue of Jufada Cresques stands in this little garden.

Cresques was the most famous of Mallorca's Jewish mapmakers who were renowned for detailed and beautiful maps. His atlas from 1375 is in the National Library of Paris.

Here he stands with a handful of maps cradled in his arms, near where the family home once stood. He was a "converso", one of the Jewish community who had to convert to Christianity.

Map 5.2 - Facing the same way as Cresques you can see the imposing Torres de Gumara with its two towers ahead of you.

Make your way towards it. Pause as you reach Carrer del Socors on your left.

Ghost Sign

Look up to see a Ghost Sign, an old, faded advertisement. This one is for Pepsi-Cola. You can just about make out the Pepsi bottle.

Map 5.3 – Continue towards Torres de Gumara.

Torres de Gumara

This building is known locally as The Temple.

It was part of a much larger fortress owned by the Gumara family and it formed part of the city wall. At one time it had eleven towers rather than the two you see today.

After the Christian conquest King Jaime I gave the fortress to the Knights Templar, and it was their headquarters until they were disbanded. It was then given to their more peaceful brothers, The Knights of St John.

It has been used for various purposes over the centuries. It was used as a prison by the Inquisition and was where Jewish converts who were suspected of only pretending to be Christian were tortured to find out "the truth".

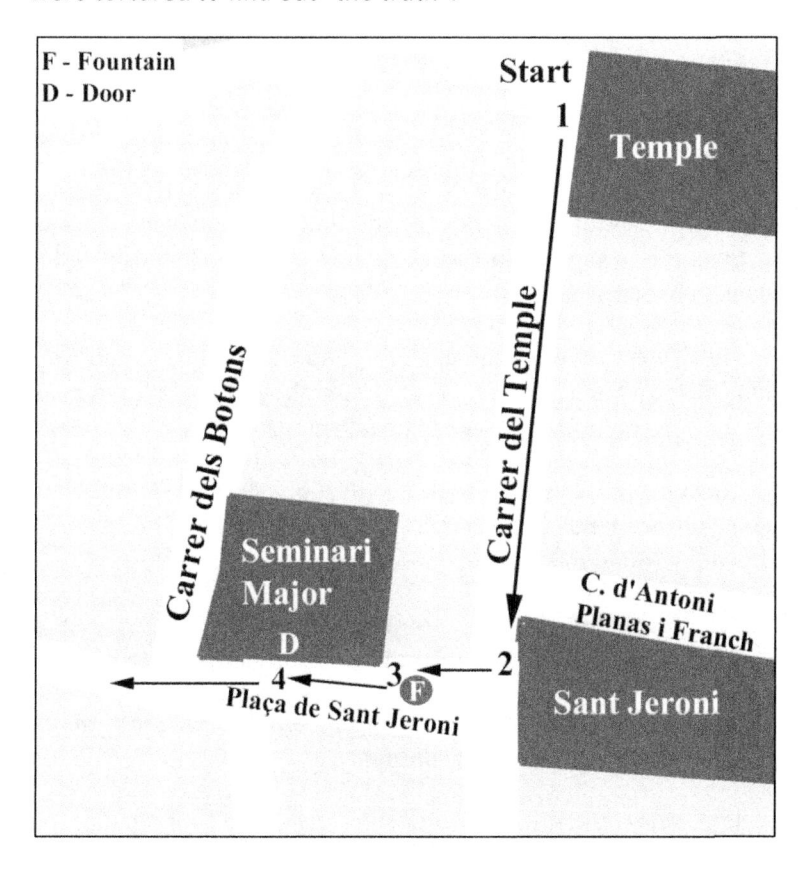

Map 6

Map 6.1 - Facing The Temple, turn right to walk down Carrer del Temple.

Pass Carrer d'Antoni Planas i Franch on your left, and you will walk into peaceful Plaça de Sant Jeroni on your right.

Plaça de Sant Jeroni

This square is another boundary of the Call Major, and it's thought a market used to be held here.

On your left as you enter the square is an old church.

Convent of Sant Jeroni

This has been the site of a religious building since the early fourteenth century. It's thought the first residents were a group of Beguines, women who were deeply religious but who didn't want to become nuns.

They were eventually evicted, and it became a convent dedicated to Saint Jerome. That is him above the door, showing off the sore on his leg for which he is famous.

The nuns survived through all the upheavals of Palma's and Spain's history, but eventually they departed in 2015 because the convent needed restoration. So, at the moment it is closed.

Its colourful mosaics were moved to the Diocesan Museum of Mallorca long ago. So, you might have seen them on Walk 1.

Map 6.2 – With the church door behind you, walk across Plaça de Sant Jeroni to the fountain.

It's a fine fountain with water spouting out of four heads.

Map 6.3 – Continue to cross the square. The ornate door you see on your right as you do, is the entrance to the Seminari Major de Mallorca.

Seminari Major de Mallorca

Just to the right of the main door you can read:

> Antic Col·legi de la Sapiència
> Former College of Wisdom

The college was founded in the seventeenth century to provide an education to the poor who wanted to train as priests. It's said that every village in Mallorca could send one pupil to the college. Palma, being much bigger could send two pupils.

Above the door you can see a medallion. It shows the Virgin Mary with Baby Jesus, and below them stands Ramon Llull on the left, and the college founder, Bartomeu Llull, on the right.

In 1985 it became the main Seminary and was until recently where Mallorca's trainee priests studied. They vacated in 2023 and at the time of writing it is not known what will happen to this historical building.

Map 6.4 – With the Seminary door behind you, turn right. Climb the steps and pass Carrer dels Botons on your right.

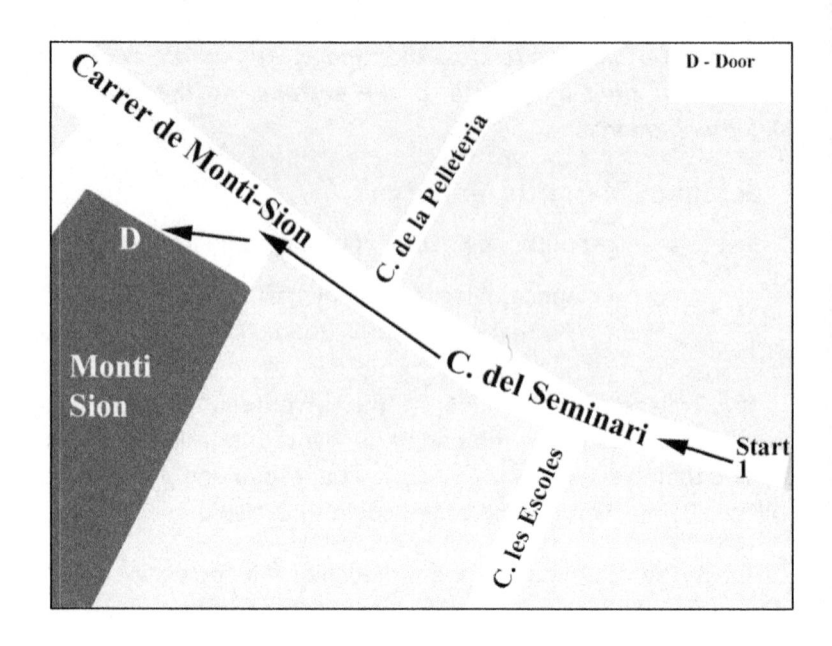

Map 7

***Map 7.1** - Pass Carrer les Escoles on your left and Carrer de la Pelleteria on your right.*

At the next little square on your left, you will find Església de Monti-Sion.

Monti Sion

This church was built over one of the two known synagogues in Palma from long ago. The one which stood here was particularly magnificent.

The Jesuits arrived in Palma and built their new church as a display of power.

Its most interesting feature is the splendidly over-the-top doorway. Those columns with a spiral running up them are called Solomon columns, and these are the only ones on the island.

Above the door is a large coat of arms, and on its left and right stand the first Jesuit saints, Ignatius of Loyola on the left and Francis Xavier on the right.

Mallorca forced its Jewish population to convert to Christianity, so officially there have been no Jews in Mallorca since the fifteenth century. However, in 1987 the first synagogue was built in Palma since that time, so the community survives, even if it's very small.

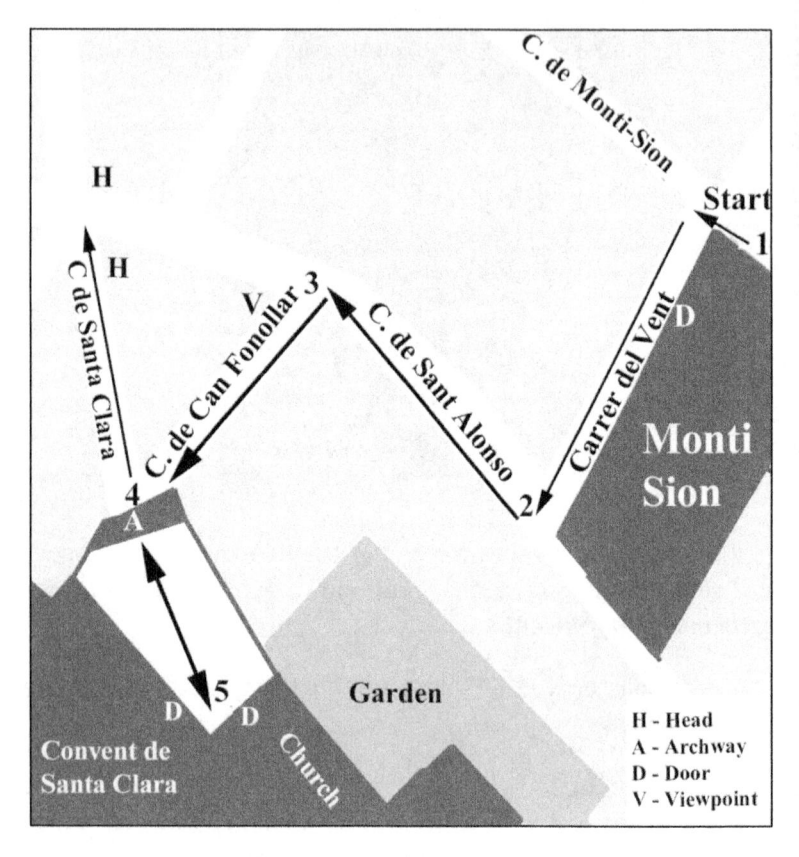

Map 8

Map 8.1 - With the church door behind you, turn left and then left again into Carrer del Vent, the street of the wind.

Carrer del Vent

As you might have guessed, the street gets its name from the constant breeze which travels through this lane. Of course there is a legend.

Just a few steps down Carrer del Vent, you should be able to make out the outline of an old door on the church wall on your left.

The legend tells us that the devil claimed the souls of the parishioners, so Jesus told him to take the souls of anyone who left by the side door. Off went the devil to wait for his prey, while Jesus stopped anyone from leaving by the side door. The devil was so angry that he raised a gale and vowed it would never leave this street.

You will reach a T junction with Carrer de Sant Alonso.

Map 8.2 - Turn right to walk along Carrer de Sant Alonso. Pause at the corner of Carrer de Can Fonollar on the left.

Viewpoint to Where

Take a second to admire the beautiful art nouveau viewing balcony on the corner. It has florally decorated stonework and a stone and wrought-iron balcony at the top. You have to ask yourself though, what were its residents viewing to merit all that expense?

Map 8.3 - Now go down Carrer de Can Fonollar.

Map 8.4 - At the bottom of Carrer de Can Fonollar you will find an archway on your left. Go through it to reach the Convent of Santa Clara.

Convent de Santa Clara

The 'Poor Clares' arrived in Palma after the Christian conquest by invitation of Pope Alexander IV and started their convent in the thirteenth century. The convent was built on a Moorish house and the diggers have unearthed a waterwheel and some tombs.

You will find yourself in a courtyard. From the archway the garden is on the left, and the church is straight ahead through an ornate door guarded by Santa Clara d'Assisi.

There are still nuns in residence in the convent, but the church is open to the public. Visit the church if it's open - if you are lucky, you will hear the nuns singing, out of sight of course.

Eggs

It's traditional for couples to visit this church the day before their wedding, give a gift of eggs to the nuns, and receive a blessing which should avoid any rain on their big day.

The nuns had so many eggs that they started making biscuits to sell back to their visitors. So, you can buy some of their traditional sweets and biscuits. Go through the door to the right of the main church door. Find the torno, a turnstile in a window. Press the bell and a nun will speak to you from behind the turnstile to take your order. Put your money in the turnstile and she will twirl it round with your sweets. Try the bocaditos de almendra (almond nibbles) or rollitos de anís (aniseed rolls).

Map 8.5 - When you are ready to move on, return through the archway and walk up Carrer de Santa Clara which is directly in front of you.

You will reach a 5-way crossroads.

Ceramic Heads

Before moving on, spot the two little heads on the walls of Carrer de Santa Clara and Carrer de San Alfonso. They were put there by ceramic artist Jaume Roig - you might spot others as you explore.

A - Archway
H - Head
B - Bridge

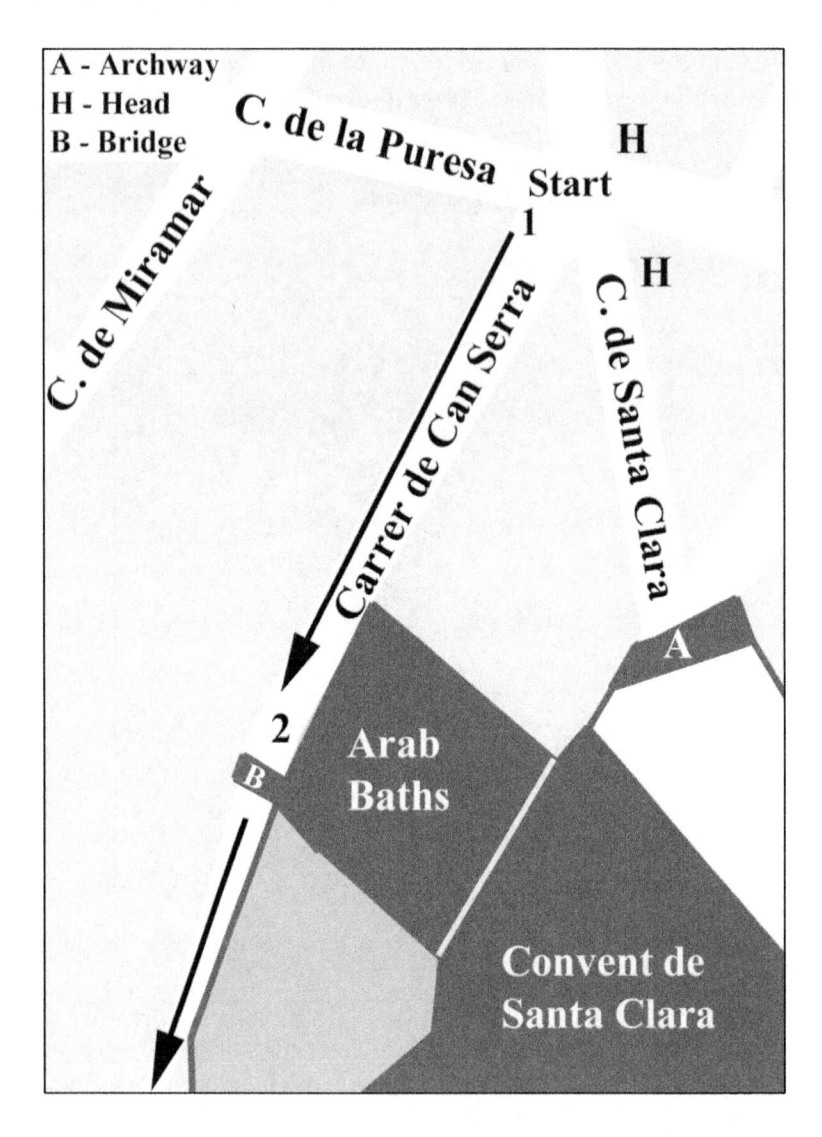

Map 9

Map 9.1 - From Carrer de Santa Clara, turn sharply left to leave the junction by Carrer de Can Serra.

You will reach the Arab Baths on your left.

Arab Baths

The baths are in a Moorish building which belonged to an Arab nobleman. It's a rare survivor from the ninth century. They stand in a lovely garden with palm trees and lemon trees where you can take a rest from exploring.

The tepidarium is the highlight, a dome punched by twenty-five openings to let the light stream in and supported by ancient columns. The columns were recycled from earlier civilisations both Roman and Muslim

Map 9.2 - Continue down Carrer de Can Senna. Walk under a little bridge joining the buildings on either side.

You will see the trees of the Arab Baths garden leaning over the wall on your left.

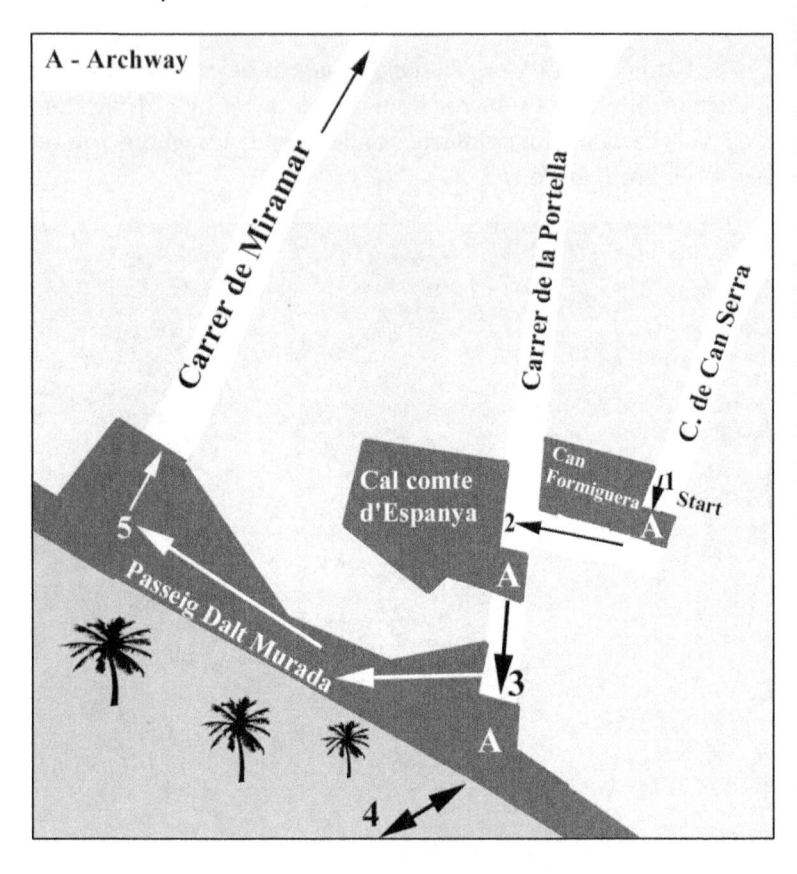

Map 10

Map 10.1 - Just after another archway the road will turn sharply right.

As you turn right you will see a short gloomy stairway with a coat of arms at the top on your right. That building is called Can Formiguera.

Walk along the side of Can Formiguera and into Carrer de la Portella.

Can Formiguera

This large house with its walk-round balcony, was thought to be one of the most luxurious houses in Palma in the seventeenth century.

Just above the balcony on the corner you can see the family coat of arms of the second Count of Formiguera, Ramon Burgues-Safortesa y Fuster.

He was a despotic and vicious young man. He tried to govern the county of Santa Margarita as a medieval fiefdom under his absolute rule. The people who lived there bravely stood up to him and took him to the courts, but there was a lot of bloodshed and death before the courts finally decided in favour of the people.

So the Count was nicknamed Comte Mal – after a legendary figure who rode a black horse breathing flames from his eyes and mouth as punishment for his sins, which included seducing a nun. There is even a folksong about him.

Opposite Can Formigeura on Carrer de la Portella is Cal Comte d'Espanya.

Cal Comte d'Espanya

This building was originally home to some Carthusian monks, an order founded by San Bru who came from Cologne in Germany. It's now in private hands but San Bru still stands guard above the ancient wooden door.

Map 10.2 - Face Cal Comte d'Espanya and turn left.

You will see an archway on the left and a gateway on the right. The gateway is sometimes open but ignore it and go through the archway.

You will find yourself just behind the city wall. In front of you is the Porta de la Portella.

Porta de la Portella

Map 10.3 - Pop through to reach the palm filled terrace and the little lake that lies between Palma and the sea.

If you walk to the lakeside, you will get a splendid view of the Cathedral and the fountain beneath it.

Map 10.4 - Return through the Porta de la Portella and turn left to climb and then walk along the top of the wall.

Map 10.5 - Take the first right, Carrer de Miramar, to head back into town.

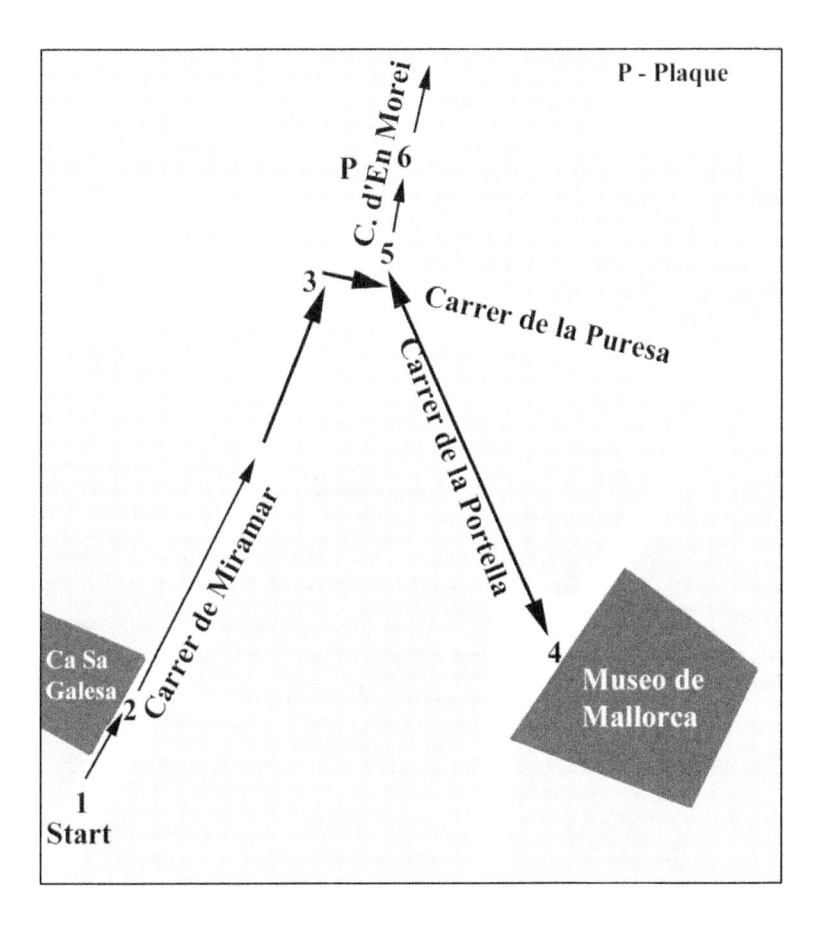

Map 11

Map 11.1 - Continue to number 8 on your left.

This is another sixteenth century townhouse which has been turned into a hotel, the Ca Sa Galesa. You can peep into its lovely courtyard.

Map 11.2 – Continue to another five-way junction.

If you don't wish to visit the Museum of Mallorca, jump to "To the Bookshop" on page 138.

Map 11.3 – Otherwise turn sharply right into Carrer del la Portella. Walk to the next junction.

You will find an arched gate leading into the Museum of Mallorca on your left.

Museu de Mallorca

The museum is in another lovely building adorned with iron balconies. It was built on top of an even older structure, thought to be one of the city's oldest Arab houses.

The building is now known as the Casa de la Gran Cristiana, the House of the Great Christian Woman. It gets that odd name from a very devout woman who lived here in the nineteenth century called Doña Catalina Zaforteza. As well as being devout, she was also very rich and involved in the labyrinth of Spanish politics – and consequently she made many powerful enemies. She was finally arrested and exiled to the west coast of Mallorca.

If you venture in, you can browse around all sorts of archeological artefacts from Palma's history – including the mysterious Talaiotic people who lived in Mallorca in the Iron Age. There are also many Roman, Moorish, and Christian pieces.

Map 11.4 – When you exit the museum, return up Carrer del la Portella back to the 5-way junction.

To the Bookshop

Map 11.5 – Orientate yourself to stand facing Carrer d'En Morei. Walk straight ahead into Carrer d'En Morei.

Just a few steps will bring you to number 14 on your left. Spot the plaque which marks this house as the birthplace of Maria Antònia Salvà i Ripoll.

Maria Antònia Salvà i Ripoll

Who? She is not someone you are likely to have heard of unless you speak Catalan. She was born in 1869 and was the first female poet to write in the Catalan language. Since she succeeded in the totally male-dominated world of her time, her birthplace and plaque are worth a short pause.

Map 11.6 – Continue along Carrer d'En Morei.

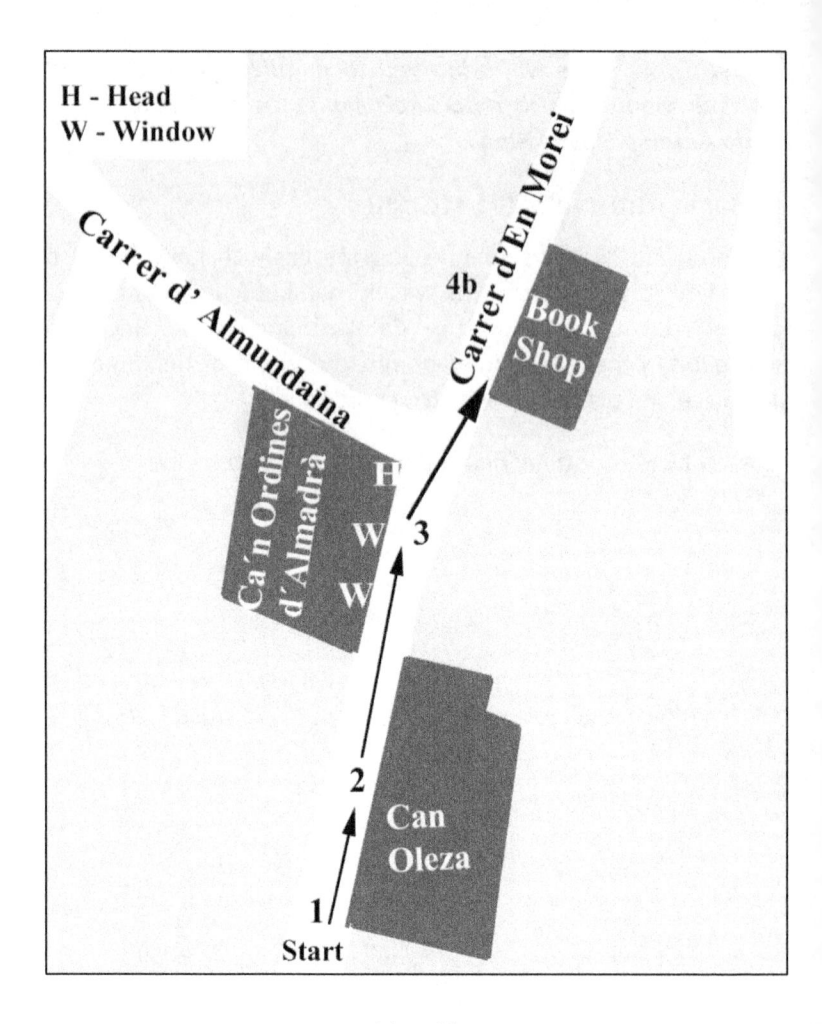

Map 12

***Map 12.1** – You will soon reach Can Oleza on your right at number 9.*

Can Oleza

If you are lucky, it will be open and you can pop in to see the lovely courtyard, but it's often closed.

This building was built by one of the oldest Mallorcan families, the Descós family. You can see their coat of arms above the windows on the ground floor. The building's style and design were copied repeatedly by Palma's noble families, and you have seen many incarnations of it as you've explored.

Map 12.2 - Continue along Carrer d'En Morei and you will find Can Ordines d´Almadrà at number 8 on your left.

Can Ordines d´Almadrà

This house isn't generally open, which is a great pity.

You can admire the single handsome Gothic window, which is topped with two rather weatherworn savages, and which sits between the doors.

Between the balconies is another very pretty window which is a reproduction installed in the twentieth century.

It's a shame you cannot visit the house as it has an intriguing courtyard. Above one of the doors there is a sculpture of two well-dressed ladies holding their index fingers to their lips – with the very sexist inscription:

Tu nube atque tace. Donant arcana cylindros

which means:

Marry and be quiet. Silence will bring you jewels

It's also home to one of the few Roman remains in Palma, a tombstone on the wall from the Roman necropolis which is known as Ara Manila. It was dug up during the 1940s when the house was renovated.

There is also another odd little face of a man at the corner of Carrer d' Almundaina.

Map 12.3 – Pass Carrer d' Almundaina on your left. A little further on and on the right is The English Bookshop. Its just opposite number 4b.

English Bookshop

The English owner moved his entire business from England to Palma. Until recently new and old books were packed into every space in the shop in a seemingly random order, inviting customers to come in and explore.

The original owner retired recently, and the new owner has brought order to the chaos.

So, although it's no longer a challenge to explore the bookshop, if you love books and like just browsing it's an interesting place to spend some time.

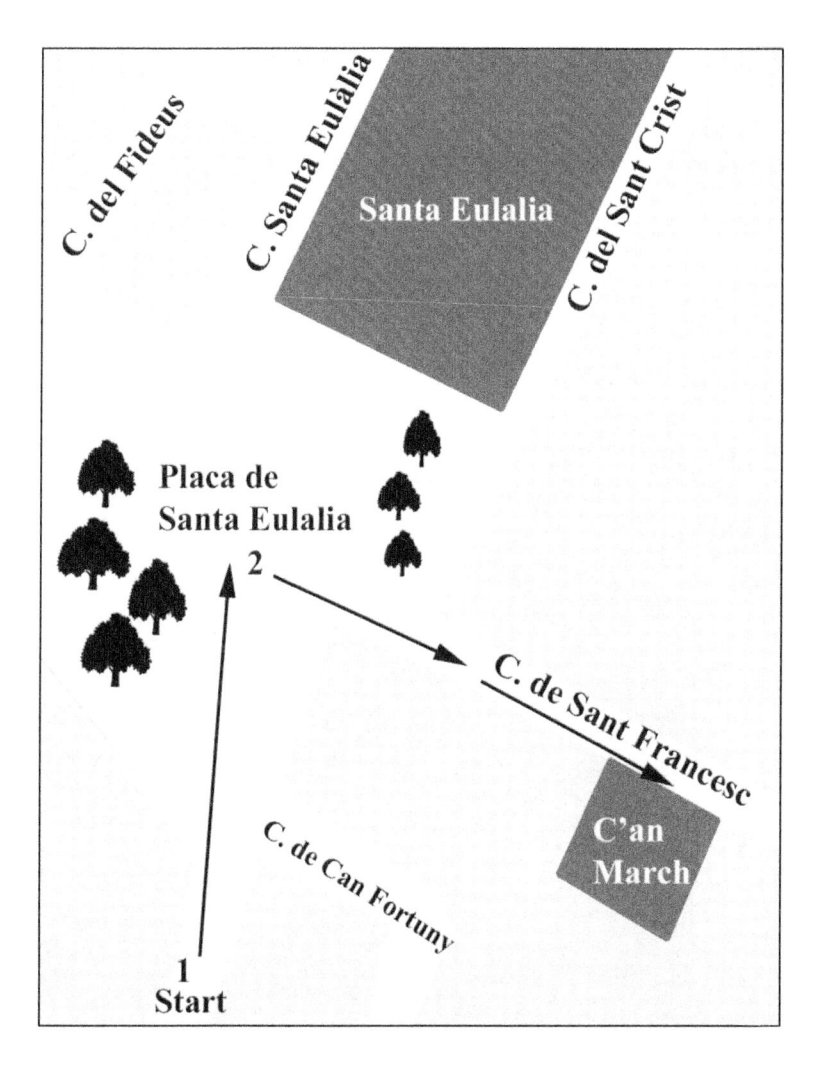

Map 13

Map 13.1 – With the bookshop door behind you, turn right to continue along Carrer d'En Morei. You will walk into Plaça de Santa Eulàlia once more.

You have reached the end of this walk.

Map 13.2 – If you would like a refreshment, you could turn right along Carrer Convent Sant Francesc.

Ca'n March

At number 8 on your right is Ca'n March, another of Palma's lovely townhouses built around a courtyard.

At the time of writing the building is a hotel and the courtyard holds a nice café, so if you feel the need for some refreshments, you could consider it.

Did you enjoy these walks?

I do hope you found these walks both fun and interesting, and I would love your feedback. If you have any comments, either good or bad, please review this book.

You could also drop me a line on my amazon web page.

Index

A

Arab Baths, 133
Arc de l'Almudaina, 94
Arc de la Drassana, 102

B

Bartolomé March Foundation, 23

C

Ca'n March, 144
Cal Comte de la Cova, 119
Cal Comte d'Espanya, 136
Cal Marquès del Palmer, 120
Call Maior, 79
Can Barcelo, 116
Can Belloto, 31
Can Berga, 43
Can Bordils, 95
Can Catlar del Llorer, 113
Can Corbella, 91
Can Formiguera, 135
Can Frasquet, 41
Can Joan de s'Aigo, 114
Can Oleza, 141
Can Ordines d'Almadrà, 141
Can Vivot, 112
Carrer de l'Argenteria, 80
Carrer de Santa Eulàlia, 82
Carrer del Vent, 129
Casa de les Mitges, 79
Casal Balaguer, 35
Casal Solleric, 31
Casasayas Building, 42
Churches
    Convent de Santa Clara, 130
    Convent of Sant Jeroni, 124
    Mont Sion, 127
    Oratori de Sant Felieu, 30
    Palma Cathedral, 8
    Sant Antoniet, 59
    Sant Francesc, 116
    Sant Miquel, 53
    Sant Nicolau, 39
    Santa Caterina de Sena, 62, 64
    Santa Eulalia, 83
Convent de Santa Clara, 130
Convent Frares Caputxins, 68
Convent of Sant Jeroni, 124
Costa de la Seu, 24

D

Dona Cosint, 71

E

El Águila, 77
English Bookshop, 142
Es Foner, 107

F

Font de les Tortugues, 34
Forn des Teatre, 48
Forn Fondo, 36
Forteza Rey, 78

G

Gaspar Bennazar Barometer, 66
Gaudi
    Casa de les Mitges, 79
    Forteza Rey, 78
    Mallorcan Modernism, 5
    Palma Cathedral, 8

Gran Hotel, 46

H

Holy Rock, 40
Hospital de sant Pere i sant Bernat, 97

J

Jafuda Cresques, 121
Jardí del Bisbe, 96
Jaume 1, 65
Jaume Roig, 131
Jonica, 108
Junipero Serra, 118

L

La Rambla, 51
L'Almudaina, 21
Llotja de Mallorca, 105

M

March Foundation, 72
Maria Antònia Salvà i Ripoll, 139
Miro
    Miro's Wall, 102
    Miro's Egg, 26
Mont Sion, 127
Monument a la Dona, 26
Museu de Mallorca, 138
Museu Diocesà, 98

N

Nancy, 110
Nu, 49

O

Olivar Market, 68
Olivo de Cort, 90
Oratori de Sant Felieu, 30

P

Palma Cathedral, **8**
Passeig des Born, 28
Pension Menorquina, 42
Plaça d'en Coll, 80
Plaça d'Espanaya, 64
Plaça de la Mare de Déu de la Salut, 58
Plaça de la Pescateria, 88
Plaça de Quadrado, 115
Plaça de Sant Jeroni, 124
Plaça de Santa Eulalia, 85
Plaça del Mercat, 38
Plaça del Rei Joan Carles I, 33
Plaça Major, 74
Porta de la Portella, 136
Porta de Santa Margalida, 62
Puerta de los Judíos, 92

R

Ramon Llull, 54

S

Sant Antoniet, 59
Sant Antoniet de Vana, 60
Sant Francesc, 116
Sant Miquel, 53
Sant Nicolau, 39
Santa Caterina de Sena, 62, 64
Santa Eulalia, 83
Sefarad symbol, 119
Seminari Major de Mallorca, 125
S'Hort del Rei, 107

T

Teatro Principal, 50
Tomas Vila, 69
Torre dels Caps, 24
Torres de Gumara, 122
Town hall, 88

U

Urbs, 75

V

Virgen de la Salud, 56

Printed in Great Britain
by Amazon